T0089302

THE LITTLE BOOK OF

BRIDGE

LEARN HOW TO PLAY, SCORE, AND WIN

BRENT MANLEY

ADAMS MEDIA
NEW YORK   LONDON   TORONTO   SYDNEY   NEW DELHI

Adams Media
An Imprint of Simon & Schuster, Inc.
57 Littlefield Street
Avon, Massachusetts 02322

Copyright © 2018 by Simon & Schuster, Inc.

All rights reserved, including the right to reproduce this book or portions thereof in any form whatsoever. For information address Adams Media Subsidiary Rights Department, 1230 Avenue of the Americas, New York, NY 10020.

First Adams Media hardcover edition June 2018

ADAMS MEDIA and colophon are trademarks of Simon & Schuster.

For information about special discounts for bulk purchases, please contact Simon & Schuster Special Sales at 1-866-506-1949 or business@simonandschuster.com.

The Simon & Schuster Speakers Bureau can bring authors to your live event. For more information or to book an event contact the Simon & Schuster Speakers Bureau at 1-866-248-3049 or visit our website at www.simonspeakers.com.

Interior design by Colleen Cunningham

Manufactured in China

10 9 8 7 6 5 4 3 2 1

Library of Congress Cataloging-in-Publication Data
Manley, Brent, author.
The little book of bridge / Brent Manley.
Avon, Massachusetts: Adams Media, 2018.
Includes bibliographical references and index.
Series: The little book of.
LCCN 2017058994 (print) | LCCN 2018000877 (ebook) | ISBN 9781507207994 (hc) | ISBN 9781507208007 (ebook)
LCSH: Contract bridge. | BISAC: GAMES / Card Games / Bridge. | GAMES / Reference. | GAMES / Card Games / General.
LCC GV1282.3 (ebook) | LCC GV1282.3 .M3416 2018 (print) | DDC 795.41/5--dc23
LC record available at https://lccn.loc.gov/2017058994

ISBN 978-1-5072-0799-4
ISBN 978-1-5072-0800-7 (ebook)

Many of the designations used by manufacturers and sellers to distinguish their products are claimed as trademarks. Where those designations appear in this book and Simon & Schuster, Inc., was aware of a trademark claim, the designations have been printed with initial capital letters.

Contains material adapted from the following title published by Adams Media, an Imprint of Simon & Schuster, Inc.: *The Everything® Bridge Book, 2nd Edition* by Brent Manley, copyright © 2009, ISBN 978-1-60550-123-9.

CONTENTS

PART 3. THE PLAY OF THE HAND // 105

PART 4. DUPLICATE BRIDGE AND RESOURCES FOR FURTHER STUDY // 137

INTRODUCTION

Are you looking for something that will stimulate your mind, provide hours of entertainment, open you to connections with new friends, and give you a hobby you can pursue for a lifetime? Congratulations! You are about to become a bridge player.

You'll join millions of people around the world who enjoy this exciting hobby. This book will get you to the first level of bridge—how it works (it's not difficult), its "language" (the bidding), and how to play your cards for the best results. You will take advantage of the at-a-glance "cheat sheet" to help you with your decisions as you play.

One of the first things you'll learn is that bridge is fun—complex without being scary. In nearly fifty years of playing bridge and three decades writing about it, I often tell those considering bridge that people of all skill levels can enjoy the game.

No matter what level you're playing at, bridge challenges your mind. As you gain experience, you will see that successful play involves puzzle solving: who has what cards, based on clues you get from what's happening at the table.

In addition to the intellectual stimulation it brings, bridge is a great way to meet new people. Even if you have just a basic understanding of bridge, there are opportunities for you to play in tournaments and clubs—the most fun way to play bridge—all over North America and even the world. You'll have all the conversation and advice you want. Or you can play at home with your friends or family. Bridge really brings people together.

I'm still learning, and that's one of the reasons I keep playing. You won't be sorry if you "follow suit" in your effort—guided by this book—to learn this wonderful game. Welcome aboard!

PART 1

BRIDGE BASICS

CHAPTER 1

INTRODUCTION TO THE GAME

Playing bridge provides a wonderful opportunity to meet people in a recreational environment where you can socialize and stimulate your intellect. Among all card games, bridge is unique. Your imagination and deductive reasoning will take you far if you let them.

Bridge has enjoyed a renaissance in the past decade as an increasing number of young professionals, empty nesters, baby boomers, and seniors have discovered the challenges and pleasures of the game. Bridge is attractive to so many players nowadays in part because it's not necessary to be an expert to enjoy the game. New players quickly learn the social aspects of organized games.

There are more than 3,200 bridge clubs in North America, and with a bit of advance notice, most are very welcoming to visitors and often provide partners. For a list of clubs, visit www.acbl.org. From your own home, to the Internet, to the bridge club, to cruise ships, to organized tournaments on the local, regional, and national level, you will find bridge to be the vehicle for meeting new friends who share your growing interest in this fascinating game.

Develop Your Communication Skills

As you learn from this book and develop your skills at bridge, you will find your communication and social skills advancing. The game of bridge may seem daunting at first, but you will soon become quite at ease with the buzzwords of bridge. You will find yourself fascinated with the endless possibilities, the excitement of your triumphs, and, believe it or not, even some of your failures. Just about every aspect of bridge has something interesting about it.

Meet New People

As you learn to play, bridge will provide many opportunities for making new friends. You will find that those who share a passion for the game have a special bond that is easily recognized. Bridge is played all over the world, and you can make new friends at clubs, tournaments, and cruises.

On the Internet, you can meet and play with people from distant lands who share your interest in the game. With dozens of free and pay sites, you can choose when to play at a moment's notice. If you want to play for only a few rounds, go ahead. But more likely you will find yourself engrossed in the game for hours at a time.

> Many aspects of bridge are not intuitive, so don't give up if one or more parts of the game come to you slower than you would like. Always keep a positive attitude and accept that lack of success is not failure. It is just a critical part of learning.

If you prefer a more organized setting and the face-to-face bridge experience, try one of the more than three thousand bridge clubs affiliated with the American Contract Bridge League. These clubs are run by friendly, welcoming people who are excited each time they encounter a prospective new member or out-of-town visitor.

Use Your Intellect and Sharpen Your Memory

You and your partner will experience different situations with each round of bridge. The multitasking skills that are required to successfully play bridge help exercise your mind and keep your intellect nimble and quick. You will learn methods for winning in this book, and with each hand you will apply those methods to win more points than your opponents. That is what bridge is all about.

Bridge is great exercise for the mind. You must train yourself to follow the cards, keeping track of who played what, who showed out of a suit, and how many cards in that suit the other players hold. You will become a bridge detective, putting together clues from the bidding and play that can lead you to the right action. Getting it right through a process of deductive logic is one of the most rewarding aspects of the game.

> The very best resource for bridge players is the American Contract Bridge League, located in Horn Lake, Mississippi, near Memphis, Tennessee (www.acbl.org or 1-800-264-2743). The ACBL staff can answer your questions, help you find bridge clubs or tournaments, inform you how to contact a bridge teacher, send you a sample of their monthly magazine if you are not a member, and sign you up on the spot if you want to join.

Getting Started: Bridge Basics

There are two phases of bridge. In the first phase, one card is dealt to each of the four players in turn until all the cards are dealt. Each player will have thirteen cards. Then the auction begins, with the dealer speaking first. This is the first phase, and there is more about this part of the game in Chapter 2. For now, just know that you and your partner compete against the other two players, who are also partners. You will be vying for the right to name one of the suits as the wild suit ("trump" in bridge lingo) in the second phase of the game. You can also bid to play without a trump suit. In addition, you are competing in the auction by raising the number of tricks you and your partner will propose to win.

Suits

A standard deck includes fifty-two cards (not counting the two jokers, which aren't used in bridge). The cards include four different suits, which are represented by symbols throughout this book: spades are represented by ♠, hearts by ♥, diamonds by ♦, and clubs by ♣. You will quickly understand the charts that represent the cards a particular player is holding in his or her hand. Note that the placement of the suit symbol is important. For example, 4 ♦ is a bid, while ♦ 4 is a card.

CARD SYMBOLS CHART	
REPRESENTATION	**ACTUAL CARDS**
♠ AKJ84	ACE, KING, JACK, 8, 4
♥ Q1085	QUEEN, 10, 8, 5
♦ 83	8, 3
♣ K10	KING, 10

The suits are always represented in the order of spades on top, hearts next, then diamonds, and finally clubs. They are in this order because spades is the highest-ranking suit and clubs is the lowest. In the auction, the order of the bids from lowest to highest is clubs, diamonds, hearts, spades, and no-trump (NT). During the auction, you and your partner will try to name a suit as the trump suit when, collectively, you have at least eight cards in that suit. You and your partner may also want to play the contract without a trump suit. Then you are playing no-trump.

The declared trump suit beats all other suits. For example, if clubs is the trump suit, a club (even a very low one) will beat any diamond, heart, or spade. This is why the ability to name the trump suit is important.

The proprieties of bridge demand that spoken communication with your partner is limited to pass, the numbers 1 through 7, the names of the four suits, no-trump, double, and redouble. All other words are strictly forbidden, as are gestures and other means of conveying pleasure or displeasure with your partner's bids or plays.

Be a Good Partner

Perhaps the most important bridge skill you can cultivate is being a good partner. If you are known as a calm, supportive partner, you will be in demand at the bridge table, even if you never become an expert.

No one wants to sit across the table from an enemy. You already have two of them at the table. If your partner is also an antagonist, you are in deep trouble. Your chances of enjoying the most enjoyable of games will dwindle sharply. As you become more keenly interested in bridge and its many nuances, you will thirst for improvement and knowledge. You must remember, however, that players progress at different paces. You might well learn more rapidly than your partner. Be patient and supportive.

How to Use This Book

For starters, beware of information overload. Don't try to absorb everything all at once. It will be easier, of course, if you have experience at card games, possibly even at bridge. For example, if you ever played the card game Spades, you already know about tricks.

It's the bidding that will take some study and concentration. Keep in mind that most experts consider bidding to be, by far, the most important aspect of the game. No matter how well you play, if you consistently fail to get to the right contract, your results will suffer.

Many of the principles of bidding are not intuitive, and there are many rules of bidding covered in later chapters. If that sounds intimidating, don't be concerned. Once you absorb the basics, it will all become clear. The key is to take each section slowly, making sure you understand the underlying principles.

Online Play and Resources

The convenience of playing online has converted many players from regular club habitués to chronic computer contestants. There are dozens of games played every week on the three main bridge websites (see Chapter 10), and it's fair to say you can play any time of the day or night online.

You don't have to play in a structured game, however. You and your partner can simply invite two other players to join you at a table, and you play until you need to stop—half a dozen deals or one hundred. It's up to you.

The Internet is also a resource for learning from the best players in the world. Most of the major matches—certainly the world championships— can be viewed live on Bridge Base Online (see Chapter 10). There is also a complete record of the bidding and play for review later if you can't or don't want to stay up to watch a bridge match in, say, China or Europe.

You also can take bridge classes online and consult with experts about your problem hands and bidding systems, and there are numerous websites with an incredible amount of information for improving your game.

CHAPTER 2

KEY POINTS TO GET STARTED

In this chapter you'll learn the basics of how to play bridge: the terms used in the game, how the cards are dealt, the hierarchy of suits, and the mechanics of play and scoring.

Bridge Jargon

Let's start with some terms that will come up over and over again in this book. Some of them may seem strange, even inexplicable. Don't worry. They will become second nature quicker than you think. Most of them are in the Glossary at the end of this book, but some additional explanation can help you get started.

- **Trick.** Four cards played in clockwise succession by each of the four players, starting at trick one with a card from the player to the left of the declarer (the player who first named the denomination of the final contract) and later starting with the player who won the previous trick. There are thirteen tricks in the play of each deal.
- **Irregularity.** New players, especially at duplicate, will encounter this aspect of bridge—a mistake in procedure—more often than others. An irregularity can be a lead out of turn, an exposed card, an insufficient bid—the list goes on. In social bridge, these errors are usually overlooked. In a club game or tournament, the director must make a ruling by consulting the Laws of Duplicate Bridge.

Becoming familiar with these terms will help you feel more at ease in a bridge setting, especially if it is a tournament or a club game. As part of your effort to study the game, make the Laws of Contract Bridge (different from the laws of duplicate) part of your library of bridge books.

It is important for your development as a player to learn the correct way to play the game. You don't want to be branded as a coffeehouser—a player with dubious ethics. The term comes from the bridge play at European coffeehouses, where conversation was often designed to give information or to guide partners in ways that are frowned upon.

A Quick Summary

In each suit, the highest-ranking card is the ace. The lowest is the 2. In the bidding phase of the game, the suits rank from the lowest, clubs, to diamonds, hearts, and spades (the highest). The cards are dealt in clockwise rotation, one to each player, until all the cards are dealt. Each player will hold thirteen cards.

The player who dealt the cards begins the auction, which proceeds clockwise. Each player in turn must bid, pass, double (only after an opponent's bid), or redouble (only after an opponent's double). Some of these terms may seem mysterious at this point, but don't worry. They will soon be clarified.

Each bid is an offer by the bidding side to win a certain number of the thirteen available tricks. A player can propose a contract in a suit, in which case that suit becomes trump and can be used to control the other suits. It is also possible to play without a trump suit. Contracts of this kind are called "no-trump" contracts. In the hierarchy of the auction, no-trump even outranks spades.

Starters

The auction begins when the dealer makes a call, which can include a pass. A deal is considered passed out when there are four consecutive passes at the beginning of the auction—in other words, when no one has a hand she or he feels confident enough to bid. The cards should be dealt again, the deal passing to the next player in the rotation—e.g., from North to East.

When you have two decks, one can be shuffled while the dealer is distributing the cards. Then the second deck is ready to go at the completion of the first deal.

Let's Play

You have a partner in bridge who sits opposite you at the table. The people to your left and right are also partners, but they are your opponents. Your opponents might be lovely people away from the table, but when you play bridge, they are the opposition and your goal is to score more points than them. That doesn't mean you should be rude or hostile. They are your friends, after all, and bridge is just a game. It's important to always maintain that perspective.

First you must shuffle and deal the cards. The dealer, sometimes determined by a cut of the cards, distributes the cards in clockwise rotation, starting with the player on his left, and continues until all fifty-two cards are dealt.

It's important to shuffle the cards thoroughly to achieve a truly random deal. Believe it or not, this topic has been the subject of a scientific study in Great Britain, where it was determined that seven is the "perfect" number of times to shuffle the cards before dealing them.

Once you have received your cards from the dealer, sort them so you can clearly see them. Most people alternate the black and red suits to keep them straight. There's nothing more embarrassing than having to admit that your "ace of diamonds" was actually a heart.

Bid 'Em Up

Once all players have their cards sorted, start the bidding. The auction, of course, is essential. Without the bidding there is no contract. Without the contract, there is no play. We will take the phases one at a time, starting with the bidding.

Each player will have at least one chance to bid, and in many deals there will be a spirited competition for the final contract.

To illustrate an auction, here is a representation. After the cards have been dealt, the dealer starts, or "opens," the bidding. The auction has begun.

West, North, East, and South

The compass points are used to identify players at the table. You could be any of the positions. North and South are always partners and sit opposite each other at the table, as do East and West, who are the second set of partners.

Each auction starts with a call by the dealer. Remember that a call can be a pass. If any person bids before there are four passes at the outset of the auction, the bidding continues until there are three consecutive passes.

How the Bidding Works

In the auction, each bid must represent a number or suit higher than the previous one. For example, a bid of 1 ♠ cannot be followed by the bid of one of any of the other suits. If someone bids 1 ♠ and you want to mention hearts, you must bid at least 2 ♥. You can, of course, bid a higher-ranking suit at the one level, as when 1 ♣ is followed by a bid of 1 ♦, 1 ♥, or 1 ♠.

If someone bids 1 ♣ and the next person bids 1 ♠, then the bid will be won by the person who bid 1 ♠ because spades are ranked higher than clubs. If the next person bids 2 ♣, that is sufficient to be a legal bid because a bid requiring a larger number of tricks always beats a bid of a smaller number.

Rank Rules

If the number of tricks is equal, the higher suit beats the lower. Once the auction starts it continues for three straight passes. The last bid becomes the contract, and the suit that was bid becomes trump.

If you win the contract, you and your partner must take at least six tricks (called the book) plus the number of tricks you bid to win the auction. For instance, if you won the auction at 3 ♥, you and your partner must collectively win nine tricks (book plus three).

> The side that "wins" the auction has an advantage because they usually have decided on the trump suit that best fits their hands, giving them a good chance for a positive score. When a trump suit has been named, those cards can keep the opponents' high cards from winning precious tricks. The other side of the equation, of course, is that there is a penalty when you do not take the number of tricks required by your contract.

Sometimes a "victory" in the auction can be a loss for your side. Bidding can be a delicate process, and some guesswork is often needed. You will notice as you get into the game that the more experienced players make accurate guesses more often than their less-skilled counterparts. In bridge, as in other aspects of life, experience is the best teacher.

If your opponents don't think you can successfully fill your contract (that is, take the number of tricks you say you can), they can *double*. This will increase your penalties when you fail to make the contract. If you disagree with the opponents' opinion of your contract, you can *redouble*, which greatly increases your score if you are right. You should be cautious about redoubling, however, because if you do fail, the penalty is greatly increased. We'll discuss the specifics of this when we come to talk about scoring.

Listen Closely

Every opening bid has a meaning that is conveyed to everyone at the table. Because it is important for partners to communicate well, players tend to bid as accurately as possible. You can take advantage of that information as you formulate your own plans. For example, say an opponent opens 1 ♠ and her partner raises her to 2 ♠.

Most people play five-card major openings (that is, they promise five cards in the suit they bid), so the opener has at least five. Players rarely raise their partners with fewer than three trumps, so now you know the opponents have at least eight spades between them. If you are looking at four low spades in your hand, you can just about count on your partner to have one spade at most, possibly none. You can use this information in deciding whether to compete—and all you had to do was listen to the bidding.

> The final bid of the auction becomes the contract for the number of tricks to be won by the winning pair after three consecutive passes end the bidding. The first player of the winning pair to have named the suit or no-trump in the contract becomes the "declarer" and takes the starring role in the next phase of the game—the play.

You and your partner will use information from the auction to decide which suit to bid and how high to compete if the high-card strength is evenly distributed between the two sides.

The bids in the auction also convey the message about the ability to win tricks and points in the second phase of the game. In most social bridge games, the bidding is oral—players speak their bids.

To help you remember the rank of the suits, place them in alphabetical order: clubs, diamonds, hearts, and spades. The lowest bid is 1 ♣, the highest is 7NT (no-trump). It's impossible—and illegal—to bid more than seven of a suit or no-trump because seven plus six equals thirteen, the total number of tricks available.

The Bidding Ladder

Take a look at the following bidding ladder. You can see that the lowest bid is 1 ♣. The first person to bid can start the auction with a bid of 1 ♣ or any higher bid. Each following bidder must make a bid that is higher on the bidding ladder; otherwise, the player must pass.

BID VALUES INCREASE AS YOU MOVE UP AND TO THE RIGHT				
7 ♣	7 ♦	7 ♥	7 ♠	7NT
6 ♣	6 ♦	6 ♥	6 ♠	6NT
5 ♣	5 ♦	5 ♥	5 ♠	5NT
4 ♣	4 ♦	4 ♥	4 ♠	4NT
3 ♣	3 ♦	3 ♥	3 ♠	3NT
2 ♣	2 ♦	2 ♥	2 ♠	2NT
1 ♣	1 ♦	1 ♥	1 ♠	1NT

At the end of the auction the final bid will be the contract. The contract will state what suit, if any, will be the trump suit, and what goal you will try to achieve in the second phase of the game when you will play the hand.

How You Play a Contract

Once the final contract is determined, the second stage of bridge begins: the play of the cards. Each partnership will try to win as many tricks as possible. The contract will state how many tricks you or your opponents will attempt to make and what suit, if any, will be trump. If you succeed in the second phase of the game, do well in the play of the hand, and make your contract, you will win points. If you are unsuccessful, your opponents will win points.

To begin, the person to the left of the declarer will play any card, usually facedown—in case that person is confused about whose lead it is. Once she is assured it is her lead, the opening leader places her card face up on the table.

At that point, the declarer's partner puts his hand down on the table for all to see. This is called the "dummy." (Not a disparaging term, just bridge lingo.) The declarer's partner arranges the cards in suits, usually alternating black and red cards. If the declarer is playing a trump contract, the trump suit goes on the declarer's far left, dummy's far right.

Touch and Go

Play proceeds in a clockwise rotation. If everyone follows suit to the opening lead, the highest card played wins the trick. Whoever wins the trick takes those four cards and puts them together in front of him.

Each player will try to win tricks for her side. If your partner is winning the trick, it would be wasteful to try to win it yourself, as when your partner has led the king of a suit and you have the ace. You know the king is going to win. You would play the ace only in the most extreme and unusual circumstance. Of course, if the ace is the only card in that suit that you hold, you must play it, wasteful or not.

If the declarer is playing a trump contract and leads a suit you are out of, you can win that trick with your lowest trump. You and your partner do not have to win a trick. Your side can purposefully choose to lose a trick, which is a key strategy in certain situations.

Winning Points

If you make your contract, you win points. When you don't make your contract you "go down" or "go set," meaning that you are charged a penalty, which is awarded to your opponents. The penalties are accrued from tricks. The shorter you fall in your attempt to fulfill your contract, the higher the penalty for failing. That's why it's sometimes attractive for your opponents to double you. If they assume you won't make a contract of 2 ♠, for example, they may double it to ensure you are penalized even more than you would be for simply not reaching your goal of winning eight tricks (book plus two).

Your First Bridge Hand

You and your partner are sitting across from each other at the table, with your opponents to your left and right. You have sorted your hand and you hold these cards.

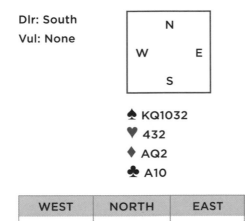

Dlr: South
Vul: None

♠ KQ1032
♥ 432
♦ AQ2
♣ A10

WEST	NORTH	EAST	SOUTH
			?

In the diagram, the suits are ranked highest to lowest. You have five cards in the spade suit. The "Vul: None" notation at the top of the diagram refers to vulnerability. This will be discussed in detail later.

Right under the card symbols are the compass points, which refer to the positions at the table. You could potentially be sitting at any of the positions, but for the purposes of this book you will be South, unless otherwise noted. As a result, your partner will be North (sitting opposite you), and your opponents would then be East and West.

Now, you ask, "Why is there a question mark under South?" Because, in this example, you (South), as the dealer, will have to decide whether or not to bid.

Your First Bid

As the dealer, you will have the opportunity to open the bidding or pass. Simply decide what you want to bid and say the words; in this case "one spade." As the dealer, or the first person with an opportunity to open the auction, there is no restriction. If you choose not to bid, you will say the word "pass." After someone bids rather than passing, ensuing bids must be higher in denomination or level.

Do you have to bid? No, you may pass if you choose as long as the auction remains open (there have not been three consecutive passes). If you pass, this conveys information to your partner that you do not have a hand that is appropriate for bidding at this time.

Let's say you bid 1 ♣. If anyone else wanted to bid, he would have to make a bid that appears higher on the chart, perhaps 1NT or 3 ♣ or 4 ♦. He cannot bid anything that appears lower on the chart, such as 1 ♥ or 1 ♦. As the auction progresses this rule still holds true. You may not make a bid that is lower than the current bid.

How long does the auction last? The auction begins with the dealer. The dealer can pass or bid. Then the next person to the left has an opportunity to bid or pass (or double—more on that later). The opportunity to bid continues around the table until each person has a turn. If all four players pass, the cards are shuffled again and a new deal starts. But if any of the four players makes a bid at his or her first turn, the auction is open. The auction then stays open until three players in a row pass.

Each time it is your turn, you may bid, pass, double, or redouble (if an opponent has doubled). If you pass at your turn, it does not prohibit you from bidding at your next turn or at any later turn.

Follow Your Instincts

Always follow your instincts when playing bridge. Let's assume you have the following cards in your hand:

♠ KQ1032
♥ 432
♦ AQ2
♣ A10

Your instinct is to make a bid. Okay, say the words "one spade." What you have essentially said is "if the next three players pass, I have proposed a contract for me and my partner to win seven of the thirteen possible tricks with spades as trumps." The biggest factor in a bridge auction is determining how much your hand is worth in the auction.

The integrity of the game requires that you make all your bids with the same cadence and inflection. The proper expression of a bid of 1 ♣ would simply be "one club." If you were to hesitate or express reluctance and say something like, "Oh, well, I think I will bid one club," then improper information might be conveyed to your partner. This is a big no-no.

Playing the Dummy

Here is your hand from the previous discussion, this time accompanied by the dummy.

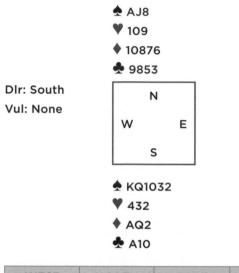

♠ AJ8
♥ 109
♦ 10876
♣ 9853

Dlr: South
Vul: None

N
W   E
S

♠ KQ1032
♥ 432
♦ AQ2
♣ A10

WEST	NORTH	EAST	SOUTH
			1 ♠
Pass	Pass	Pass	

The auction is over because you (South) opened the bidding with 1 ♠, followed by three passes. West makes the opening lead of a low club. Now the spotlight turns to you.

Everyone has a minute or so to look at the dummy. The play of the cards continues clockwise around the table. The next card will be played from dummy, and you, as the declarer, will decide what card to play from dummy. When you decide, you pick a card or tell the dummy what card to play. Your right-hand opponent will play a card to the trick and then you will follow. A club was led and you do have a club in dummy, so you must play a club. You will play the ♣ 3 from dummy and your right-hand opponent will play a club, almost certainly a face card. You, as declarer, will play last to this trick. You will play the ♣ A. You have won the trick from your hand, so you are required to lead the first card to the next trick from your hand. If you had won the trick with a card you played from the dummy's hand, you would play the first card from dummy in the next trick.

Before you lead, think for just a moment. Look at just the spades in the two hands combined. This is the trump suit, and because of that, you will want to take control of the suit. The reason is simple. You have five spades in your hand and three in dummy. That is a total of eight of the thirteen spades in the suit.

Make a Plan

You know that your opponents have only five spades between them. Now look at your spade suit from your perspective as declarer and count the number of tricks you can win in that suit. When you pull all the trumps out of the opponents' hands, you alone will have trumps remaining.

Whenever you are playing a hand, either as declarer or as one of the defenders, take some time before you play a card to the first trick. Look at your hand and dummy and give some thought to the auction. It is important to make a plan. Remember, even a plan that fails is better than no plan at all.

On your first bridge hand, you can absolutely make seven tricks and succeed at your contract. You will win five spade tricks, the ace of clubs, and the ace of diamonds for a total of seven tricks. You will make your contract.

Scoring

In all forms of the game, players receive rewards for meeting their contracts. Players receive scores based on how many "odd" tricks they take.

An odd trick is any trick in excess of the "book," or first six tricks. In other words, if you bid 2 ♠, you are contracting to take two odd tricks. If you do so on the nose, you receive 60 points.

If your contract is in a minor suit (clubs or diamonds), you receive 20 points for each odd trick you take. If it's a major suit (spades or hearts), you receive 30 points per odd trick. If you play in no-trump, the first odd trick is worth 40 points, and subsequent odd tricks are 30 points each.

Both sides are striving to achieve 100 points to make "game," and most party or rubber bridge games are played to win two out of three games. Party bridge games have scoring "above the line" and "below the line." To achieve a game score, you must have 100 points below the line.

Points below the line are achieved only through successful contracts—and only for the number of tricks contracted for. That is, if you contract for 2 ♠ and take nine tricks, you get 60 points below the line (the two odd tricks you contracted for) and 30 above (the overtrick). If you win the auction on the next deal and play 2 ♠ again, making your contract, you score another 60 points below the line. The total exceeds 100, so you have achieved game. If you do that again, you win the rubber.

If you double the opponents and defeat them in their contract, the premium for defeating the contract goes above the line. It does not count toward your game bonus; nor does the bonus for making slam (taking twelve or thirteen tricks).

If you take twelve tricks in the hand, that is called a small slam. Taking all thirteen tricks is a grand slam. Both entitle you to a bonus: a small slam earns 500 points; a grand slam is worth 1,000 points.

Of course, you can get your game bonus in one fell swoop by simply bidding "game" in a major (4 ♥ or 4 ♠), a minor (5 ♣ or 5 ♦), or 3NT. You also get credit for game if you bid a slam. Your slam bonus goes above the line, however.

When you have a score of less than 100 below the line, you are considered to have a "leg" toward your game bonus.

Double Your Fun

You now know a bit about the mechanics of the auction—bids, passes, and other calls—if not the actual meanings of the bids, but what is doubling and redoubling?

You will learn more about doubling in later chapters. For now, it's important to know that when one player doubles an opponent, it's because the doubler thinks the opponent has bid too much, and she wants to increase the penalty for failing to make the contract.

If the opponent who has been doubled has confidence in his bidding, he can redouble, increasing the bonus for making the contract. When there is doubling and redoubling going on, someone has made a big mistake. Finding out who made the blunder is part of the excitement of the game.

There are many meanings of double in the parlance of bridge, especially in the world of tournaments. The most common non-penalty double is the so-called takeout double. That's when one player opens in suit and the player in the next seat says "double." The doubler is asking his partner to "take out" the double by bidding his best suit.

After a double or redouble, if another player makes a bid of any denomination, the double or redouble is canceled.

Scoring in duplicate bridge (discussed in Chapter 9) is quite different from the scoring in social games.

In duplicate bridge, each score you achieve is separate from all the other scores. You do not add up trick scores to make your game. If you don't bid to the game level, you don't get credit for it. If you do bid and make game, however, you get a bonus right away—an extra 300 points if you are not vulnerable and an extra 500 if you are. You also get credit for the overtricks. So if you bid 4 ♠ and make eleven tricks (you needed only ten), you get plus 150 points for the five odd tricks and another 300 if you are not vulnerable, for a total of 450 points. Check the Glossary for more on vulnerability.

PART 2

BIDDING, THE LANGUAGE OF BRIDGE

CHAPTER 3

COMMUNICATING AT THE TABLE

Bridge is a game of tricks, and accurate card play is paramount to success, but if you consistently find yourself in a poor contract, it won't matter if you can play the spots off the cards. It is well known that two average players in tune with each other in the bidding often have an advantage over two experts with sketchy communication. If you want to succeed, learn to bid.

Choosing a Bidding System

Before you begin playing bridge, you have to decide on a system for evaluating your hand so you know what to bid. Let's start with a basic point-count system.

You can thank Milton Work for his pioneering efforts in developing the language of bidding and for helping give the bridge world one of its most basic tools—the point count. Work, a Philadelphia lawyer and expert whist player, eventually left the practice of law and took up bridge as his profession in the early part of the twentieth century (he died in 1934). Work was instrumental in publicizing the point-count method of hand evaluation that is still used today. The method was developed by an obscure player named Bryant McCampbell, but it is known as the Work point-count method because it was through Work's writings that the system gained almost universal acceptance. The method is very simple. You evaluate your hand on a points system, with the following parameters.

CARD POINT VALUE	
Ace	4
King	3
Queen	2
Jack	1

Using this scheme, each suit has 10 high-card points, so a deck has 40 altogether. The average bridge hand has about 10 points.

> Many bridge authorities consider the Work point-count method to be flawed. For example, in the context of a 4-3-2-1 method of high-card evaluation, most experts consider the ace to be worth more than 4 points, and a jack fewer than 1. Nevertheless, the Work system is the one used by just about everyone in bridge today.

How does this apply to the language of bidding? Well, while you were counting your points, your partner was doing the same, and it is through the bidding that the two of you will exchange information about the relative strengths of your two hands. Your objective is to reach the best contract, be it a part score, game, or slam. A part score is a bid that, if successful, will produce fewer than enough points for game—for example, 2 ♠ (you must bid 4 ♠ for game).

Bare Minimums

If you are the dealer, you will have the first chance to speak. When you pick up your hand and sort it into suits, you then count your high-card points. You are trying to decide whether you should open the bidding. If you do, what does that mean? A simple opening bid conveys a lot about the thirteen cards you are holding in your hand.

> The bidding presented in this book is the system known as Standard American. There are other systems used by some tournament players and a variety of systems played primarily in other countries. Learning Standard American will put you in a great position to play with anyone in North America.

High-Card Points and Their Importance

Opening bids come in a variety of flavors, so to speak, and it's logical to start with the one level. Here are all five bids you can make at the one level and what they tell your partner about your hand (please note, HCP is an abbreviation for high-card points):

- 1NT: 15–17 HCP, balanced.
- 1♠: 12–21 HCP, five or more spades, may be balanced or unbalanced.
- 1♥: 12–21 HCP, five or more hearts, may be balanced or unbalanced.
- 1♦: 12–21 HCP, probably more or better diamonds than clubs, may be balanced or unbalanced. In any case, a minimum of three diamonds.
- 1♣: 12–21 HCP, three or more clubs, may be balanced or unbalanced.

You noted, no doubt, the reference to "balanced" in each of the descriptions of one-level opening bids. A hand is considered balanced if it has one of three shapes: 4-3-3-3, 4-4-3-2, or 5-3-3-2. Here are some examples:

♠ KQ103	♠ K732	♠ KQ1093
♥ 1092	♥ QJ92	♥ QJ2
♦ A92	♦ A92	♦ A92
♣ A65	♣ A10	♣ A4

The first has four cards in spades and three cards in each of the other suits. The second has four spades, four hearts, three diamonds, and two clubs. The last has five spades, three hearts, three diamonds, and two clubs.

Note that none of the hands has more than one doubleton (that is, only two cards in a single suit). These are considered balanced hands. Any other pattern is described as unbalanced, although some players consider any hand without a singleton (one card in a suit) to be at least a little bit balanced. As you progress in your experience and learn more about the game, you will form your own opinions on this subject. For now, best to stick to the rules as they are written here.

Just for practice, count the high-card points in each of the example hands. Did you get 13, 14, and 16 points, respectively, for the three hands? Excellent! For the record, each is a fine opening bid.

In bridge language, a doubleton is a holding of just two cards in a suit. A singleton, naturally, is one card in a suit, sometimes identified as a stiff because it's more or less "dead"—it must be played the first time the suit is led. When you have no cards in a particular suit, you are said to be void.

Twelve Is Enough

You will note that the one-bids of a suit in the list of openers gave a minimum high-card point count of 12 for opening bids of one of a suit. If you and your partner are more comfortable with setting your minimum at 13 high-card points, you will do just fine, but most players today open with 12, and even fewer when a hand is very "shapely," that is with two long suits. Experience teaches that shapely hands play very well when your partner has support for one or both of them.

The reason for discussing the issue of what constitutes a minimum opening bid, at least in terms of high-card points, is that when you open, your partner will have to decide what message to send you about her hand.

Remember, the reason for the exchange of information between partners is to determine how high the bidding should go. For example, if you have an opening hand yourself and your partner opens the bidding, you will get to game in some denomination almost all of the time—and expect to make it with normal breaks in the key suits.

In figuring whether to go for a part score, game, or slam, keep these general guidelines in mind. To make game in 3NT—you must take nine tricks without trump cards to help you out—usually requires about 25 high-card points between the two hands. The same goes for game in a major suit (spades or hearts), which requires ten tricks but with the assistance of your trumps. Game in a minor suit (diamonds or clubs), on the other hand, requires eleven tricks, so you need 27 or 28 high-card points or some extra distribution.

Every Bid (or Pass) Communicates

Once your partner opens the bidding, if the next player passes, it's up to you to begin describing your hand.

You will hold a variety of hand types, each of which will require different treatment. Your hands will vary in strength as well, another facet you must communicate to your partner. Bear in mind that once your partner has revealed something about his hand—most descriptively by opening one of a major—your assessment of your hand will be expressed in "support points," a combination of your high-card points and, if you have support for the suit your partner has opened, any distributional values you might have, such as doubletons, singletons, or voids.

When your partner opens one of a suit and you have at least three-card support for a major or four-card support for a minor, you can count points for short suits. Traditionally, with four-card trump support for the partner's major, you can count 1 point for a doubleton in a side suit, 3 support points for a singleton, and 5 for a void. With three-card support for a major, count no extra for a doubleton, 1 for a singleton, and 2 for a void.

Assuming the partner has opened at the one level, there are four kinds of hands you will have to describe:

- Bad hand: Usually fewer than 6 HCP. Pass tells your story.
- Minimum strength: Usually 6–9 HCP, perhaps a "bad" 10.
- Medium strength: Usually a "good" 10 to a "bad" 12 points.
- Game-forcing strength: A hand with which you probably would have opened the bidding yourself, possibly even more.

The matter of "good" and "bad" points is worth addressing. Good points are aces and kings, four-card support (or better) for your partner's major-suit opener, and suits with good intermediate cards (9s and 10s). "Bad" points are in hands with dull shape, three-card support, and high-card points in queens and jacks, especially doubleton queens and tripleton jacks. Some experts go so far as to add value to a hand that has no jacks.

In the parlance of bridge, a two-card holding of a queen and a jack is a "quack," an especially dubious value considering that it represents 3 high-card points that might not take a trick. Beware of quacks in evaluating your hand.

Your response when your partner opens the bidding at the one level depends in large measure on what the opening bid was. The most descriptive one-level opening bid is 1NT, which requires a completely different set of responses. That leaves the openings of 1 ♣, 1 ♦, 1 ♥, and 1 ♠, which, as has been noted, have a very wide range, from as little as 12 high-card points to as many as 20 or 21.

Major or Minor Opening?

Responder's choices differ greatly depending on whether the opener started with a major or a minor. If the opening was 1 ♣ or 1 ♦, the responder's first priority is to attempt to locate a major-suit fit with the opener. Most bidding systems are designed for that purpose.

If the responder has a major suit of four cards or longer, she will simply bid that suit at the one level. A bid of 1 ♥ in response to an opening of 1 ♣ has a very wide range, from as little as 6 high-card points to a true monster. All the opener knows after the responder bids 1 ♥ is that the responder has four or more hearts. At that point, the responder has said nothing about the strength of her hand except that she had enough to respond (at least 6 high-card points).

When your partner opens one of a minor, you will focus on your major suits when formulating your response.

- With one four-card major, bid it. You would, of course, bid the suit if it was longer than four cards.
- With two four-card majors, bid 1 ♥. That does not deny four spades, and it allows opener, should he have four spades but not four hearts, to continue describing his hand by bidding 1 ♠. You can raise to the appropriate level at your next turn.
- With five of one major and four in the other, bid the longer suit.
- With five cards in each major, start with 1 ♠. You may have a chance to bid hearts later to show your second suit.
- With six cards in a major, bid it. You plan to rebid your suit later (the stronger your hand, the more you will bid at your second turn).
- With a balanced hand, no four-card or longer major, and 6–9 HCP, bid 1NT. If partner's opening was 1 ♣ and you have four or more diamonds, you might select 1 ♦ as your response instead of 1NT.

- With a balanced hand, no four-card major, and 11–12 HCP, bid 2NT.
- With a balanced hand, no four-card major, and 13–15 HCP, bid 3NT.
- With an unbalanced hand, 6–9 HCP, no four-card major, and four-card or better support for partner's minor, bid two of opener's suit. This bid can be passed.
- With an unbalanced hand, 10–12 HCP, no four-card major, and four-card or better support for partner's minor, bid three of opener's suit.
- With an unbalanced hand, 13 or more HCP, no four-card major, and four-card or better support for partner's minor, make some forcing bid, perhaps 1 ♦ in response to 1 ♣ or 2 ♣ in response to 1 ♦. If your hand just isn't right for a bid of 2 ♣ over 1 ♦, you might have to bid a three-card major. Some game-forcing hands you might hold after partner opens one of a minor can be awkward to bid. Fortunately, they don't come along that often.

The Captaincy Principle

Of all the concepts you will study in learning the game of bridge, there are few more important than the captaincy principle. The concept is as simple as it is elegant: in the bidding, when one member of a partnership limits her hand, that player's partner becomes the "captain" of the auction. The captain makes the decision about how high the bidding should go.

The easiest way to illustrate the principle is to consider the auction that begins with 1NT. That is the ultimate in a limiting bid. Most players open 1NT with 15–17 high-card points. That narrow range allows the partner of the 1NT opener to make an accurate assessment of where the two hands should go. The partner of the opener is the captain and cannot be overruled in any decision he makes.

For example, if the responder to 1NT bids 2 ♥, she is indicating that she has at least five in her suit but not enough high-card points to consider going any higher than the two level. It is a sign-off bid and no matter how good the opener thinks his hand is, his only option is to pass. The responder, after all, knows about his partner's hand. The 1NT opener, however, knows nothing about his partner's hand except that he wants to play 2 ♥.

Consider the following auctions and see if you can identify the bids that limit one hand or the other.

WEST	NORTH	EAST	SOUTH
1 ♣	Pass	1 ♥	Pass
1NT			

Answer: 1 ♣ is somewhat limited, but 1 ♥ can be as little as 6 high-card points or very strong. 1NT limits the opener to 14 high-card points (if he had, say, 15, he would have opened 1NT, not 1 ♣). The 1 ♥ bidder is now the captain.

WEST	NORTH	EAST	SOUTH
1 ♠	Pass	1NT	Pass
2 ♣			

The 1 ♠ is limited in a sense (as was 1 ♣ in the first example), but still offers a wide range of possibilities. The 1NT strongly implies that the bidder does not have 10 high-card points, but that is the only limiting factor. The opener's 2 ♣ bid is limited by the failure to rebid 3 ♣, showing 18–20 high-card points, but the range for the opener's hand is still pretty wide at 12–17.

WEST	NORTH	EAST	SOUTH
1 ♦	Pass	1 ♥	Pass
2 ♥			

The 1 ♦ is limited in the same way as the other opening bids in this exercise, and 1 ♥ is not limited, but the raise to 2 ♥ definitely is. The opener is showing roughly 12–15 points in support of hearts. If any further action is to be taken, it will have to be by the responder.

Here's an example of an auction where the captaincy principle is violated. Suppose East holds this hand:

♠ QJ9
♥ J1054
♦ K763
♣ 32

Now consider this auction:

WEST	NORTH	EAST	SOUTH
1 ♠	Pass	2 ♠	Pass
Pass	3 ♣	3 ♠	

East's bid of 3 ♠ is a big no-no because it violates the captaincy principle. East limited his hand by bidding 2 ♠, and there is nothing about his hand that has changed. By limiting his hand, East made West the captain of the auction. In the given auction, it's West's decision about what to do over the 3 ♣ bid (known as "balancing" because North does not want to let the opponents play a comfortable 2 ♠). What if West's hand is something like the following?

♠ K8763
♥ A2
♦ 109
♣ KQJ9

After West hears North bid 3 ♣, she will be licking her chops in anticipation of the chance to double, expecting a juicy penalty. West will not be pleased to have that chance preempted by her partner.

Write this down and study it with your partner. Once you have described your hand, all further decisions in the auction are left to your partner.

The Importance of Shape

As you learn more about the game of bridge, you'll hear the term "shape," referring to hands. As you'll see, when it comes to shape, not all hands are equal.

Many expert players devalue hands that are "flat," and the worst shape possible is the dreaded 4-3-3-3. Unless such a hand is blessed with an abundance of high-card points, the trick-taking potential is seriously reduced. Think about it: no long suit to develop for extra tricks; no shortness that could allow for ruffs. Dull shapes, such as this one, should set off warning signals in your head.

> A play in which you take non-trump cards with a trump card is called a ruff.

Then there are the freaks—hands with extreme distribution, such as seven cards in one suit, six in another, and two voids! If you hold such a hand and find that your partner has support for one of your suits, you can take lots of tricks.

Most "shapely" hands fall somewhere between completely flat and the 7–6 freaks. A hand with five cards in each of two suits can be a big trick taker, and you will learn later in this book how to describe such hands when the opponents get the first shot in the bidding. Such hands are more common than you might think.

Rule of Twenty

The bottom line is that you can be more aggressive in the bidding when you have a shapely hand, which brings up the so-called Rule of Twenty, a notion that has gained a lot of support in recent years. Warning: the "rule" also has detractors, for reasons that will become clear.

Basically, the rule is a formula for helping you determine whether to open the bidding on hands that fall short of the 12 or 13 high-card points that most bidding systems advocate.

Here's how it works: take the number of cards in your two longest suits, then add the number of high-card points. If the sum is 20 or higher, open the bidding. Players who use this rule as a substitute for thinking or judgment are doing themselves and their partners a disservice. The Rule of Twenty is a useful guideline, but it should not be followed blindly. Here are a couple of examples to bring home the point.

♠ AJ1076
♥ AJ987
♦ 9
♣ 54

Using the Rule of Twenty, you count the high-card points (10) and add the number of cards in hearts and spades, the two long suits, and you come up with 20. This is a perfectly respectable opener, and if your partner has good support for one of your suits, you have the chance to take a lot of tricks.

Now look at the other extreme.

♠ 95432
♥ 107543
♦ AQ
♣ A

This is a poor hand for opening the bidding. The negatives are that the two long suits are very weak and that the high-card strength is in short suits. Yet this hand qualifies for the Rule of Twenty: there are 10 high-card points and 10 cards in hearts and spades. You are begging for trouble if you open this hand, however. Put the ♣ A in the spade suit and the ♦ AQ in the heart suit, and you're back in business—open 1 ♠.

Augmentation

Instead of blindly following the Rule of Twenty, some players adjust it to what they call the Rule of Twenty-Two. The same parameters are still in place, but with an additional requirement: two quick tricks (that is, tricks that can be taken without the aid of other cards—for instance, if you hold AK in a suit, you have two quick tricks). The new rule, then, is that high-card points and cards in the two long suits must add up to 20, and you can open as long as you have two quick tricks.

For reference, here is your guide to quick tricks:

TRICKS	REQUISITE HOLDING
2 Quick Tricks	AK of the same suit
1½	AQ of the same suit
1	A or KQ of the same suit
½	K and any card

The reason you want to include quick tricks in your calculation is that, in today's atmosphere of competitive bidding, if you open on a shapely hand with little or no defense (aces and kings) and your partner doubles the opponents, you will regret having opened when their contract comes rolling home. Two long suits without quick tricks will not help you on defense.

The other part of the equation is that your partner will begin to doubt your openers, so even when the opponents step out of line and your side should be doubling, your partner won't cooperate because he has seen too many bad opening bids from your side of the table. He is now gun-shy.

Minor or Major?

When you open 1 ♣ or 1 ♦, your partner's response will center on the major suits. If she has one, she will bid it. Most of the time, if your partner does not bid 1 ♥ or 1 ♠ when you open a minor, she doesn't have a four-card major. The exception is when the responder to 1 ♣ bids 1 ♦, which does not deny a four-card major.

When your partner has opened 1 ♣, you usually bid your suits "up the line." That is, bid the lowest-ranking suit (diamonds) first if you have four of them. Be careful, however, when you have a minimum responding hand with four diamonds and four hearts. In that case, it is better to bid 1 ♥. The reason is that if the next player bids 1 ♠ before your partner can make her rebid, there's a good chance you will not be able to establish a fit in hearts because neither you nor your partner will be strong enough to mention the suit at the two level.

As the opener, after you have started with one of a minor, if your partner bids one of a major, your responsibility is to describe your hand as accurately as possible. If your partner has responded 1 ♥ to your opening and you have four-card support, raise to the appropriate level. Bid 2 ♥ if you have 12–15 support points, 3 ♥ with 16–18 support points, and 4 ♥ with 19 or more support points. The same applies to a response of 1 ♠ when you have four-card support.

Here are your priorities after opening one of a minor:

- Raise partner's major to the appropriate level. Any other bid denies four-card support.
- Rebid one of a major when partner has responded 1 ♦ to your opening bid of 1 ♣.
- Rebid 1 ♠ over the response of 1 ♥ if you do not have four-card heart support.
- Rebid a six-card or longer minor suit at the two level with 12–15 HCP, at the three level with 16–18 HCP.
- Rebid a lower-ranking suit (clubs after opening 1 ♦) at the two level with a minimum to intermediate hand. Note: you can rebid 2 ♣ after opening 1 ♦ with as much as 17 HCP, just short of a jump-shift rebid.
- Rebid a lower-ranking suit at the three level (3 ♣ after opening 1 ♦) with 18–19 HCP.
- Rebid 1NT with a balanced hand of 12–14 HCP. If partner has responded 1 ♥, this denies four-card heart support. It also denies four spades.
- Rebid 2NT with a balanced hand of 18–19 HCP. This denies four-card support if partner responded 1 ♥, but it does not deny four spades. The priority in this case is to show the strength of the hand. If partner has four spades, she can bid the suit over 2NT.
- Rebid 3NT with a very strong six-card or longer minor suit, 17–19 HCP, and no support for partner's major.

Openers at the Two Level and Higher

Many of the bids at the two level are highly descriptive. Most of them are meant primarily to annoy the opponents. Here is the menu:

- 2 ♣: Your big bid, describing a powerful hand with 22 or more HCP if balanced. If unbalanced, it is a hand with lots of tricks, usually from a long, powerful suit.

- 2 ♦, 2 ♥, 2 ♠: What is known as a weak two-bid, usually describing a six-card suit and 5–10 HCP (the range can be different if you and partner prefer).

- 2NT: A balanced hand with 20–21 HCP (you can have a different range if you prefer).

- 3 ♣, 3 ♦, 3 ♥, 3 ♠: Weak hand (circumstances can dictate extreme weakness) with a long suit, usually at least seven cards.

- 3NT: A balanced hand even stronger than a 2NT opener (perhaps 24–25 HCP). Some players agree that it shows a long minor suit of at least seven cards headed by the AKQ.

- 4 ♣, 4 ♦, 4 ♥, 4 ♠: In the minors, bids at the four level usually show eight-card suits. The majors are similar, but for tactical reasons 4 ♥ or 4 ♠ can sometimes be bid on a seven-card suit.

- 5 ♣, 5 ♦: More preemption (the removal of bidding space). These are usually based on eight- or nine-card suits.

- 5 ♥, 5 ♠: Bids carrying a specific message to partner: e.g., bid six of my suit if you have one of the top-three honors; bid seven if you have two. This is not a weak bid.

Most preemptive bids are weak, and there is some risk in starting the bidding at a high level with a weak hand, but the rewards can more than compensate. Robbed of bidding space by your preemption, the opponents will often have to guess what to do. In such cases, they will guess wrong a certain percentage of the time. As pointed out earlier, experienced players guess correctly more often than newcomers, but even top players are not impervious to the havoc that can be wreaked by an opening bid of, say, 5 ♦.

Stayman

One important bidding tool you should master is Stayman (named for Sam Stayman, who first described it in 1945). It's a convention that will come up elsewhere in this book.

When your partner opens 1NT and you want to know if your side has a fit in a major suit, you bid 2 ♣. This has nothing to do with clubs (although it doesn't preclude your having several cards in clubs). It directs your partner to answer one question: do you have a four-card major?

The bid of Stayman, with one exception, requires the responder to have at least 8 high-card points. The use of Stayman does not mean that the partnership is definitely going to game, but it promises at least an invitation to that level.

Responses to Stayman

After your partner responds 2 ♣ to your 1NT opener, here are your responses:

2 ♦ = no four-card major
2 ♥ = four hearts, possibly four spades
2 ♠ = four spades but not four hearts

Why does the opener bid hearts first? It's simple. Remember, the responder promises no more than enough to invite game. So if the opener responds 2 ♥, showing four hearts and maybe four spades, the responder can bid 2 ♠ as an invitational bid with four spades. If the opener does not want to go to game, he can pass with four spades or bid 2NT without a fit in the suit. Either way, the bidding ends and the two hands are still at the two level.

Now suppose the opener bids spades first and the responder still has only the invitational hand. He would have to bid 2NT (implying four hearts, otherwise why bid Stayman?). If the opener is still minimum but has four hearts, she will have to bid at the three level when she believes the contract will play better in a suit than in no-trump. You never want to push yourself to a higher level than necessary. The opponents are already doing that, so why should you?

What kind of hand should you have to bid Stayman? See what you would do with these:

♠ AK105
♥ Q3
♦ 8753
♣ 1098

This is perfect for Stayman. If your partner bids 2 ♥, you will bid 2 ♠, showing four spades and enough to invite game. If your partner bids 2 ♦, you will show your invitational values by bidding 2NT.

♠ K4
♥ 106
♦ Q54
♣ AK5432

Unfortunately, you can't bid 2 ♣—that would ask your partner to bid a four-card major. You have 12 high-card points, plenty enough for game. Just bid 3NT. If you were thinking that 5 ♣ would be a better contract, you aren't far off. Those two wimpy hearts could be a problem, but in the long run you will be better off just blasting into 3NT.

Basically, if you want to use Stayman, you should have at least one four-card major and enough to invite game. If your hand is especially "square" (balanced), you usually won't use Stayman even if you have a four-card major. The following hand is an example.

♠ A1075
♥ A87
♦ 654
♣ K97

With this hand, bid 3NT. You have more than enough high-card points for game, so just bid it.

CHAPTER 4

YOUR FIRST AUCTION

All right! You're ready for your first auction. Let's get started.

There are fifteen words used in the auction phase:

- The numbers 1 through 7.
- The names of the four suits.
- No-trump, pass, double, and redouble.

These are the only words you are permitted to use, and you should speak them, if your bidding is oral, in an even tone without undue emphasis.

At the same time, remember that one of your objectives in the auction is to communicate the state of your hand to your partner (just as she is telling you about her hand).

> Modern bidding is designed to help partners discover when two hands have at least eight cards in the same suit (usually a major) between them. This is known in the vernacular as a "golden fit." It is highly advantageous in many cases to have four cards of the suit in each hand, providing opportunities for using the trumps separately and for generating extra tricks.

You and your partner have a distinct advantage when one of you makes the first bid of an auction. You have immediately started your exchange of information about your respective hands, and you have put the opponents at a disadvantage because there is risk involved for them if they intervene. Maintain that edge by honing your skill at communicating with your partner.

Partner's First Response

Once your partner opens the bidding, if the next player passes, it's up to you to begin describing your hand.

You will hold a variety of hand types, each of which will require different treatment. Your hands will vary in strength as well, another facet about which you must tell your partner. Bear in mind that once your partner has revealed something about his hand—most descriptively by opening one of a major—your assessment of your hand will be expressed in "support points," a combination of your high-card points and, if you have support for the suit your partner has opened, any distributional values you might have, such as doubletons, singletons, or voids.

When your partner opens one of a suit and you have at least three-card support for a major or four-card support for a minor, you can count points for short suits. Traditionally, with four-card trump support for your partner's major, you can count 1 point for a doubleton in a side suit, 3 support points for a singleton, and 5 for a void. With three-card support for a major, count no extra for a doubleton, 1 for a singleton, and 2 for a void.

Assuming your partner has opened at the one level, there are four kinds of hands you will have to describe:

- Bad hand: Usually fewer than 6 HCP. Pass tells your story.
- Minimum strength: Usually 6–9 HCP, perhaps a "bad" 10.
- Medium strength: Usually a "good" 10 to a "bad" 12 points.

- Game-forcing strength: A hand with which you probably would have opened the bidding yourself, possibly even more.

The matter of "good" and "bad" points is worth repeating. Good points are aces and kings, four-card support (or better) for a partner's major-suit opener, and suits with good intermediate cards (9s and 10s). "Bad" points are in hands with dull shape, three-card support, and high-card points in queens and jacks, especially doubleton queens and tripleton jacks. Some experts go so far as to add value to a hand that has no jacks.

Your response when your partner opens the bidding at the one level depends in large measure on what the opening bid was. The most descriptive one-level opening bid is 1NT, which requires a completely different set of responses, all of which are covered in Chapter 8.

That leaves the openings of 1 ♣, 1 ♦, 1 ♥ and 1 ♠, which, as has been noted, have a very wide range, from as little as 12 high-card points to as many as 20 or 21.

Major or Minor Opening?

The responder's choices differ greatly depending on whether the opener started with a major or a minor.

If the opening was 1 ♣ or 1 ♦, the responder's first priority is to attempt to locate a major-suit fit with the opener. Most bidding systems are designed for that purpose.

If the responder has a major suit of four cards or longer, she will simply bid that suit at the one level. A bid of 1 ♥ in response to an opening of 1 ♣ has a very wide range, from as little as 6 high-card points to a true monster. All the opener knows after the responder bids 1 ♥ is that the responder has four or more hearts. At that point, the responder has said nothing about the strength of her hand.

Many new players make the mistake of thinking they have to make some kind of strength-showing jump bid when their partner opens one of a minor and they have an opening bid as well. They somehow get the idea that a bid of 1 ♥ with 17 high-card points does not do the hand justice. They forget that when the partner opens 1 ♣ and they respond as an unpassed hand, their bid is 100 percent forcing. The opener is not allowed to pass a response from a hand that has not yet passed.

When your partner opens one of a minor, in formulating your response you will focus on your major suits.

- With one four-card major, bid it.
- With two four-card majors, bid 1 ♥. That does not deny four spades, and it allows opener, should he have four spades but not four hearts, to continue describing his hand by bidding 1 ♠. You can raise to the appropriate level at your next turn.
- With five of one major and four in the other, bid the longer suit.
- With five cards in each major, start with 1 ♠. You may have a chance to bid hearts later to show your second suit.
- With six cards in a major, bid it. You plan to rebid your suit later (the stronger your hand, the more you will bid at your second turn).
- With a balanced hand, no four-card or longer major, and 6–9 HCP, bid 1NT. If partner's opening was 1 ♣ and you have four or more diamonds, you might select 1 ♦ as your response instead of 1NT.
- With a balanced hand, no four-card major, and 11–12 HCP, bid 2NT.
- With a balanced hand, no four-card major, and 13–15 HCP, bid 3NT.
- With an unbalanced hand, 6–9 HCP, no four-card major, and four-card or better support for partner's minor, bid two of opener's suit.
- With an unbalanced hand, 10–12 HCP, no four-card major, and four-card or better support for partner's minor, bid three of opener's suit.

- With an unbalanced hand, 13 or more HCP, no four-card major, and four-card or better support for partner's minor, make some forcing bid, perhaps 1 ♦ in response to 1 ♣ or 2 ♣ in response to 1 ♦. If your hand just isn't right for a bid of 2 ♣ over 1 ♦, you might have to bid a three-card major. Some game-forcing hands you will hold after partner opens one of a minor can be awkward to bid. Fortunately, they don't come along that often.

Some examples will help explain how to decide on the best bid. Partner has opened 1 ♣. What is your bid with the following hands?

♠ 987
♥ K765
♦ 8
♣ AQJ76

Bid 1 ♥. You have good support for your partner's 1 ♣ opener and 10 high-card points, but if you raise clubs first, you deny a four-card major. If your partner raises your heart suit, your hand increases in value, and it would not be outrageous to simply jump to 4 ♥. It would not be out of line, however, to simply make an invitation to game.

♠ A987
♥ K765
♦ 8
♣ AJ107

You will still bid 1 ♥. If your partner raises, you will go straight to game. If your partner bids 1 ♠, you will bid game in his suit. If he bids 1NT, denying four-card heart support and four spades, you will bid 3NT. Yes, the singleton diamond makes you nervous for play in no-trump, but if your partner can't raise hearts or bid spades, he probably has a stopper or stoppers in diamonds.

♠ 987
♥ K76
♦ 87
♣ AQJ76

Bid 3 ♣. This is a so-called limit raise, which shows 10–12 high-card points, and no four-card major, but at least four clubs. If there is a game in the offing, it will most likely be in 3NT, so do not count distributional points when making a limit raise in a minor.

♠ AJ10
♥ AKJ765
♦ K8
♣ Q4

Bid 1 ♥. You know you are going to at least game—perhaps slam—but the right place to play is not known at this point. For example, if your partner rebids in clubs, showing at least six of them, you will give serious thought to investigating a slam in clubs. Don't worry, your partner will not pass 1 ♥.

♠ QJ8
♥ KQ9
♦ 986
♣ QJ76

Bid 2NT, showing your balanced distribution and enough high-card points to invite game. You also deny a four-card major.

♠ 987
♥ 765
♦ 86
♣ AQJ76

Bid 2 ♣, the most descriptive bid you have. There are many losers, but you have too much to consider passing and 1NT is not a good choice with such weakness in three suits. If you have so much strength in the club suit, your partner should be able to cover some of your losers in the other suits.

Major Suits

When your partner's opening bid is in a major, your options are limited by the strength of your hand. Rather than making your life harder, however, that limitation makes things easier in the sense that you don't have to choose from a wide variety of bids, which can be perplexing at times.

Your first priority when your partner opens one of a major is to raise his suit. That requires at least three cards in the suit that was opened. When the opening is 1 ♥ or 1 ♠ and you have support for the suit:

- With 6–9 support points (perhaps a "bad" 10), bid two of opener's suit.
- With 10–12 support points but only three card-support, bid a side suit at the two level, planning to support partner's major suit at your next turn to bid.
- With 10–12 support points and at least four-card support for opener's major, bid directly to the three level in the major—a limit raise.
- With 13 or more HCP and support for opener's major, bid a new suit at the two level. You will judge your next bid by opener's response. If he indicates a minimum opener, you will probably sign off in game.

Handy Tool

You will find yourself using 1NT as a response to one of a major more often than you might expect, in large measure because a bid of a new suit at the two level in response to a major-suit opening requires at least 10 high-card points. Suppose your partner opens 1 ♠ and you are holding this hand:

♠ 3
♥ QJ10987
♦ K1062
♣ J7

You sense that if your side is going to play the contract, it should be played in hearts. Your partner might have a hand such as:

♠ AJ765
♥ K
♦ Q75
♣ K1083

No matter what suit your partner plays in, your hand, with that nice long heart suit, will be of almost no use to her. By contrast, if you can manage to play a heart contract, you can do pretty well. With the dummy's ♥ K to help fill out your suit, you have at least five trump tricks in your hand. Your partner's ♠ A makes six, and you can take at least one trick in diamonds by driving out the ace of that suit. You are up to seven tricks now, with at least a couple of chances for an eighth.

How do you get to 2 ♥? Your partner is never going to bid the suit, and you don't have enough high-card strength to bid 2 ♥ in response to your partner's opening bid.

The solution is to bid 1NT. With the hand shown for your partner, she will bid 2 ♣, and now you can give your partner the news by bidding 2 ♥. That bid says to your partner that you have a long heart suit (usually at least six cards), no support for her major suit, not enough strength to bid 2 ♥ directly over 1 ♠. A disciplined partner will pass, happy that she has an honor in your suit, even if it is a singleton.

Sometimes, your partner will pass 1NT, usually when she has only a five-card major and no second suit to show—in other words, 5-3-3-2 shape—and a minimum opening bid.

From your partner's perspective, when she holds such a hand, 1NT is as good a place to play as any.

Keeping It Low

When your partner's opening bid is 1 ♥ and you do not have the three-card support needed to raise his suit, at least you have one more option available to you at the one level. If you have four or more spades, you can bid 1 ♠. If your partner raises you to 2 ♠, which he will do when he has four spades, you have found a playable spot. If he rebids 1NT, that is likely to be your place to play when your response is in the minimum range (6–9 high-card points).

Bidding 1NT in response to an opener of 1 ♥ sends this message: "Partner, I don't have support for your major suit, I don't have four or more spades, and I don't have enough high-card strength to bid at the two level." That's a lot of information in one bid, which is the essence of bidding accuracy.

Opener's First Rebid

When you open the bidding and your partner responds, you have started a dialogue. At your second turn in the auction, your job is to continue the conversation by making the most descriptive bid possible.

Opening bids come in different ranges:

- Minimum: 12–15 HCP.
- Intermediate: 16–18 HCP.
- Maximum: 19–21 HCP.

Of course, there are other features of your hand that you will want to make known—extra cards in the suit you opened, perhaps a second suit. The main message you want to send, however, relates to the strength of your hand—and it is possible to send two messages with one bid.

♠ AJ10765
♥ KQ6
♦ 107
♣ K10

You open 1 ♠, to which your partner responds 1NT. You have a six-card spade suit, and you are definitely in the minimum range for your opener. You can tell your story in one bid: 2 ♠. Your partner now knows that you have an extra spade but no extra strength. Suppose, however, that your hand looks more like this:

♠ AKJ765
♥ A8
♦ AJ10
♣ 93

Now you have 17 high-card points along with your extra spade. Your proper rebid is 3 ♠, sending the message that you have at least six spades plus 16–18 high-card points.

These two examples show the principle at work, but the rank of the suit you opened can make a big difference in how you rebid.

Minor or Major?

When you open 1 ♣ or 1 ♦, your partner's response will center on the major suits. If she has one, she will bid it. Most of the time, if your partner does not bid 1 ♥ or 1 ♠ when you open a minor, she doesn't have a four-card major. The exception is when the responder to 1 ♣ bids 1 ♦, which does not deny a four-card major.

If your partner bids one of a major after you have opened with one of a minor, it is your responsibility as the opener to describe your hand as accurately as possible. If your partner has responded 1 ♥ to your opening and you have four-card support, raise to the appropriate level. Bid 2 ♥ if you have 12–15 support points, 3 ♥ with 16–18 support points, and 4 ♥ with 19 or more support points. The same applies to a response of 1 ♠ when you have four-card support.

Here are your priorities after opening one of a minor:

- Raise partner's major to the appropriate level. Any other bid denies four-card support.
- Rebid one of a major when partner has responded 1 ♦ to your opening bid of 1 ♣.
- Rebid 1 ♠ over the response of 1 ♥ if you do not have four-card heart support.
- Rebid a six-card or longer minor suit at the two level with 12–15 HCP, at the three-level with 16–18 HCP.
- Rebid a lower-ranking suit (clubs after opening 1 ♦) at the two level with a minimum to intermediate hand. Note: you can rebid 2 ♣ after opening 1 ♦ with as much as 17 HCP, just short of a jump-shift rebid.
- Rebid a lower-ranking suit at the three level (3 ♣ after opening 1 ♦) with 18–19 HCP.
- Rebid 1NT with a balanced hand of 12–14 HCP. If partner has responded 1 ♥, this denies four-card heart support. It also denies four spades.
- Rebid 2NT with a balanced hand of 18–19 HCP. This denies four-card support if partner responded 1 ♥, but it does not deny four spades. The priority in this case is to show the strength of the hand. If partner has four spades, she can bid the suit over 2NT.
- Rebid 3NT with a very strong six-card or longer minor suit, 17–19 HCP, and no support for partner's major.

The one rebid not covered in this list deserves special mention. It is a bid called a "reverse." It occurs most often after an opening of one of a minor and the response of 1 ♠. If you rebid 2 ♦ (after having opened 1 ♣) or 2 ♥ (after having opened either minor), you are showing a strong hand, usually at least 16 high-card points. The reason you must have extra strength is that if your partner has to go back to your first suit, he must do so at the three level. You don't want to be that high if you have a minimum opener and your partner has a minimum response.

Major Issues

If you have opened one of a major, you have plenty of choices for rebids, always striving to make the most descriptive rebid possible. Here are your priorities after you have opened 1 ♥ or 1 ♠ and your partner has responded:

- After opening 1 ♥, raise a response of 1 ♠ to the appropriate level with four-card support, 2 ♠ with 12–15 support points, 3 ♠ with 16–18 support points, and 4 ♠ with 19 or more support points.
- Pass with a minimum opener when partner makes a minimum or "limit" raise of your major (10–11 support points).
- Consider making a game try with an intermediate hand when partner makes a minimum raise. Bid game if partner makes a limit raise.
- Pass partner's response of 1NT with a minimum opener and a balanced hand (no side four-card suit).
- Rebid a six-card or longer suit at the two level with a minimum opener, at the three level with intermediate values.
- Raise partner's response of 1NT to 2NT with intermediate values (18 to a poor 19 HCP) and a balanced hand.
- Raise partner's response of 1NT to 3NT with maximum (good 19 to 20 HCP) and a balanced hand.
- Bid a lower-ranking side four-card suit at the cheapest level with a minimum to intermediate opener. As noted with minor-suit openers, you can have up to 17 HCP for a rebid at the two level.
- Bid a lower-ranking suit at the three level with 18–19 HCP.

With a six-card or longer major suit and a hand that should make game when your partner responds to your opener, you can just charge into 4 ♥ or 4 ♠—but that can make it difficult to reach slam when your partner has some potentially useful cards but no bidding space to show them.

Many experienced players take this into account and get creative, perhaps making a jump-shift rebid on a three-card suit. That can provide some extra bidding room that would be lost if you simply jumped to four of your major.

This is somewhat esoteric and might be tricky for newer players, but keep it in mind and add it to your repertoire as you gain experience.

CHAPTER 5

COMPETITIVE BIDDING

In many ways bridge is like war, except with friendly opponents (it is a social game, after all). This is especially true when neither side holds a significant advantage. Both sides scratch and claw, with whatever weapons they might have at their disposal, trying to gain an advantage. In the arena of competitive bidding, the bold often hold the edge.

The Opponents Open the Bidding

The side that takes the first shot usually has the advantage, but when the opposition is well armed, it often doesn't matter who gets the first blow.

When one of your opponents opens the bidding, you have some choices:

- **Pass.** This tells your partner you have nothing to say at the present time.
- **Overcall in a suit**—as in bidding 1 ♠ after your right-hand opponent starts with 1 ♥. Your 1 ♠ bid is an overcall. Making this call generally shows a suit of five or more cards of decent quality. The overall strength of the hand should be appropriate to the level of the bid and of the vulnerability.
- **Overcall in no-trump,** usually either 1NT (showing a balanced hand, a stopper in the suit that was opened, plus 15–18 HCP) or 2NT (a conventional bid showing at least five cards in each of the two lowest unbid suits).
- **Make a cuebid of opener's suit** (as in 1 ♣—2 ♣). This is another conventional way to show two-suited hands.
- **Make a takeout double.** A direct double of an opening bid tells partner that you have the rough equivalent of an opening hand and at

least three-card support for the unbid suits. Partner is not allowed to pass unless he has a long, strong holding in opener's suit.

As you can see, there are many options available for competing. Experience will teach you to choose the right one for each different situation.

Roads Not Taken

Astute players use information about options their partners could have taken to draw inferences as the bidding and play progress. You can make deductions about your partner's hand from her failure to act on available options.

Listening to the bidding is more than just hearing the calls. Really listening means interpreting the messages and using them to your advantage.

It is usually safer to take action in the direct seat—that is, next to bid after an opponent opens—than after both opponents have bid and exchanged information. The more they know about each other's hands, the better they will handle your interference.

Principles of Overcalling

There is danger in overcalling, but there is also danger in not overcalling (you may miss a big reward).

Fasten your seatbelt, because once the opponents take the first shot, the auction is now competitive and you are in for a battle. Overcalls are your weapons in this competitive auction. You will serve a specific purpose when you make an overcall.

Why Overcall?

The following are reasons why you might want to be involved in the opponents' auction:

- To try to interfere with opponents' communication.
- To tell partner about a good suit.
- To tell partner what suit to lead if you end up as defenders.

When the opponents have opened the bidding and you have an opportunity to get in there, the direct seat may be your only chance. You will feel pretty silly if you have a legitimate one-level overcall, decide to pass, and find that the bidding is at the four level when it comes back to you. The following auction is not uncommon.

WEST	NORTH	EAST	SOUTH
1 ♥	Pass	2 ♥	Pass
4 ♥	Pass	Pass	?

Perhaps your hand was worth a 1 ♠ bid, something like:

♠ QJ987
♥ 98
♦ KJ63
♣ Q10

How do you feel about entering the auction now? It could be a disaster. Your partner might have good spade support for you, maybe even enough to make 4 ♠ or at least push the opponents one level higher, but you left your partner out of the loop with your failure to overcall. It might seem risky to bid 2 ♠ over 2 ♥ in the given auction, but when the opponents have found a fit in a suit, your side usually also has a fit in another suit. Passing over 2 ♥ can land you in the uncomfortable spot of having to decide at the four level.

Overcall Parameters

Your first goal is to tell your partner that you have a suit with lots of cards in it. For overcalls, that's usually five or more at the one level, often six or more at the two level or higher. You know that the opponents have some strength because they opened the bidding, and you also know what suit is strong for them, because you heard their bid. When you overcall, you are offering to play the hand with your strong suit as trump.

> You do not need as many points to overcall as you do to open the bidding. The hurdle for opening the bidding is 12 high-card points with adequate quick tricks or any hand with 13 or more. All you need to overcall on the one level is a good suit and 8 or more high-card points.

Your second objective in overcalling is to tell your partner what suit to lead later if the opponents win the auction. You want your partner to lead your suit.

And finally, you want to take up bidding space to try to limit the opponents' opportunity to communicate. Remember those obnoxious, preemptive three-level bids? Well, some overcalls can have the same effect. If you make an overcall, they can only use the available bids that are higher on the bidding ladder.

When the opponents open at 1 ♣ or 1 ♦, you have lots of space left on the one level and all of the higher bids. When the opponent opens a higher-ranking suit, like 1 ♥ or 1 ♠ or 1NT, you will have to be a bit more careful, but it's a bidder's game and no one promised you a rose garden. Get in there and bid when you think it's right.

Let's look at some hands that you would love to overcall when the opponents open the auction—and the reason you will make the overcall.

♠ AKJ75
♥ 87
♦ 9753
♣ 75

Your right-hand opponent opens 1 ♣. Are you game?

You can certainly get into this auction. You do not need to have as many points as the opener. The 13-point hurdle the opener has to jump over does not count for you. All you have to do is fit one or more of the criteria for joining this auction:

- 8–17 HCP and most of the points concentrated in your suit if you are at the lower end of the HCP range.
- A five-card suit.
- You have jammed the auction by bidding 1 ♠. The opponents will have to bid at least 1NT to stay in this auction. You certainly would not mind playing this hand, but even if you don't end up as declarer, you will be pleased to have your partner lead this suit if you end up as a defender.

There is, of course, a downside to overcalling. One of your opponents could have a stack in your suit, meaning you would probably be doubled. That will happen from time to time, but, as the famous quote goes, "Faint heart ne'er won fair lady."

Overcalling just to make noise is a bad policy. You should have a purpose when you get into the bidding. Ask yourself (1) whether your hand provides a reasonable shot at a plus score, (2) whether it will be helpful to your partner if you enter the auction, and (3) if it will interfere with the opponents' communication. Remember, you have told your opponents the same information you have told your partner. They will use this information against you just as you try to use the information about their bids against them.

Higher Plane

Overcalling at the one level is relatively safe because it's tough to exact a meaningful penalty against you when you need only seven tricks for your contract. The two level is vastly different territory, and you must exercise extreme caution in overcalling at the two level when you are vulnerable.

This following hand, for example, would be a reasonable overcall in diamonds if the opening bid is 1 ♣.

♠ Q64
♥ 109
♦ AKJ54
♣ 743

If the opening bid on your right is 1 ♥ or 1 ♠, however, it would be suicide to bid that five-card suit in that hand at the two level. That is not even close to a two-level overcall at any vulnerability, and it would be madness if you are vulnerable. A vulnerable two-level overcall would look more like this:

♠ 764
♥ K9
♦ AKJ1098
♣ K10

That's a bare minimum two-level vulnerable overcall.

Takeout Doubles

There are many ways to compete when an opponent opens the bidding, and a must for your bidding toolbox is the takeout double. When you double an opponent's opening bid—and that includes bids higher than one—it sends a message to your partner that you are short in the opener's suit and have at least three cards in each of the other suits. Your partner is directed to pick her best suit—sometimes "best" means longest—and bid it an appropriate level. The parameters for responding to a takeout double are covered in the next chapter.

Suppose your right-hand opponent opens 1 ♥. Which of the following hands is appropriate for a takeout double?

♠ Q1098
♥ 6
♦ AJ43
♣ KQ72

This hand has perfect shape, the requisite high-card count, and excellent support for any suit your partner might bid. This is a textbook takeout double.

♠ Q109
♥ 643
♦ AJ43
♣ KQ7

Pass is best after your right-hand opponent bids 1 ♥. The shape is the worst possible. You have what is known as the "death holding" in opener's suit and you have only three spades. When you double one major, your partner will strain to bid the other major. This is not great support. Again, your right-hand opponent has opened 1 ♥.

♠ J1098
♥ 6
♦ QJ43
♣ K872

This one has perfect shape, but is short of high cards. Pass.

♠ Q109
♥ A543

♦ AQJ4
♣ 82

One of the most common errors among beginners is making a take-out double with a hand of this kind. Yes, there are 13 high-card points, but where are the clubs? What will you do if you make a takeout double with this hand and your partner bids clubs? Pass and let him languish in a 4–2 trump fit? He won't enjoy that. Bid 2NT? That shows a hand stronger than a 1NT overcall—roughly 19 high-card points. It may be counterintuitive to pass with an opening hand, but sometimes you have to do that.

Occasionally you have the wrong shape initially but get a second chance in the bidding.

Try this one on for size.

♠ QJ109
♥ 64
♦ AQ432
♣ A2

Your right-hand opponent opens 1 ♥, and unless you feel like over-calling 1 ♠ on that four-card suit, you must pass. You can't double with this hand for the same reason you couldn't double with the previous example hand. But wait! What if the auction proceeds as follows?

WEST	NORTH	EAST	SOUTH
		1 ♥	Pass
1NT	Pass	2 ♣	?

Now you are well placed to enter the bidding with a double. There are currently only two unbid suits, and you have support for both. This is the time to double. Your partner should understand that this is for takeout, showing spades and diamonds, and she will understand from the auction why you didn't double at your first opportunity.

Other Competitive Doubles

The double has many uses in bridge besides penalty and takeout. In today's modern game, one of the most common uses for the double occurs after your side opens the bidding.

In days past, when your partner opened one of a minor and the next player bid 1 ♠, the following hand type presented a serious problem.

♠ 87
♥ QJ62
♦ KJ94
♣ J62

If your right-hand opponent had passed, you would have happily bid 1 ♥. You have more than enough to respond, and you could tell your story in one quick bid. When your right-hand opponent overcalls 1 ♠, however, you are no longer so happy. You have no spade stopper, so 1NT won't work, and raising your partner to 2 ♣ with that anemic holding has little appeal. Well, what about hearts or diamonds? To bid either of those suits, you will have to go to the two level, which requires a minimum of five cards.

Furthermore, you have only 8 high-card points, and bidding at the two level shows at least 10.

This kind of hand is the reason that Alvin Roth, one of the all-time great players, invented a tool that has become a staple of just about every bidding system worldwide.

It's called the negative double, with the "negative" stuck in there to, you might say, "negate" the penalty aspect, because it's not meant to punish the opponent for a bad bidding decision. It's for takeout.

In the formative years of bridge, a double after an opponent's overcall was for penalty, but you don't get many chances for a significant penalty of a one bid. Roth, one of the great bidding theorists of all time, reasoned that the double in the given situation was more useful as a way to show the other two suits.

> The negative double was originally known as the Sputnik double because when Roth and his partner, Tobias Stone, introduced the new bidding device in 1957, the Russian space satellite was getting a lot of publicity. The negative double is still known as the Sputnik double in some countries.

Here's how it works. When your partner opens one of a suit—usually a minor—and the next player overcalls, a double indicates that you have enough to respond and, usually, that you have four-card support for the unbid suits.

With negative doubles, the emphasis is always on the majors. This is the formula:

- When an opening of 1 ♣ or 1 ♦ is overcalled by 1 ♠, double usually shows a four-card heart suit and probably—but not necessarily—four or more cards in the other minor.
- When an opening of 1 ♣ or 1 ♦ is overcalled by 1 ♥, a bid of 1 ♠ shows at least five spades. With only four spades and enough to respond, employ the negative double.
- If 1 ♦ is overcalled by 2 ♣, double indicates possession of at least one four-card major.
- The negative double can be used when you hold a suit longer than four cards but without the 10 HCP needed to bid at the two level. You can double, and if partner bids your suit, decide whether to raise or just pass. If partner bids some other suit, you can bid your long

suit to reveal the nature of your hand and the reason for the negative double.

- There is no upper limit in terms of HCP for a negative double, although most of the time you will have a relatively modest hand. You could, however, have a strong hand but choose to use the negative double to find a fit in a major suit. The negative double is one of the handiest of the conventions you will learn as you progress. It has almost universal acceptance.

How High?

When the opener's rebid in response to a negative double will be at the one or two level, assuming the next player passes, you can make a negative double on minimum values, roughly 6–9 high-card points. If the opener will have to bid higher than the two level, the high-card-point requirements for a negative double will increase.

Discuss with your partner how high the opponents can bid before negative doubles become penalty doubles. Most experienced partnerships agree that negative doubles are in effect through the three level. That is, if your partner opens one of a minor and the next player bids 3 ♠, double is still for takeout. Of course, when you are forcing your partner to bid at the four level, you must have a strong hand.

Information, Please

One of the best uses of the double is to help your partner out with his opening lead. Suppose your left-hand opponent opens 1NT and, after your partner passes, your right-hand opponent (RHO) bids 2 ♣, a conventional bid called Stayman. It is completely artificial and is used to inquire of the opener whether he has a four-card major.

Bridge writers frequently use terminology and jargon that may be unfamiliar to newer players. The notation RHO signifies your right-hand opponent and LHO your left-hand opponent.

Now, suppose your holding in clubs is something along the lines of KQ1098. It certainly appears likely that the opponents are going to end up playing the contract, and if the 1NT opener bids a major suit that is raised by his partner, that means your partner will be on lead. So, what suit do you think will be the best lead for your side? That's right! You want your partner to lead a club.

How do you get your partner to cooperate? You double. When you double an artificial bid, it shows that you have length and strength in the suit. So if your partner finds himself on opening lead, he should start with a club unless he has a great excuse, such as being void in the suit.

If you play in tournaments, you will encounter many artificial—not to say esoteric—bids that give you the opportunity to help your partner with his opening lead, or even find a suit that you and your partner can bid as a way of competing.

> Be careful about doubling artificial bids if it is likely you are going to be on lead against the final contract—as when it is clear your right-hand opponent is going to play a spade contract and she has bid some suit you can double. Doubling gives the opponents a chance to exchange more information, and you could be providing the declarer with potentially useful information.

- **Jacoby.** Transfers over 1NT and 2NT. In the simplest form, bidding diamonds asks opener to bid hearts; bidding hearts asks opener to bid spades. Transfers are useful because they keep the stronger hand concealed—an advantage in most cases.
- **Stayman.** Already mentioned.
- **Gerber.** An ace-asking convention of 4 ♣.
- **Responses to the 4NT (Blackwood) convention,** also asking for aces.

There are many other artificial bids. The key is to be aware of the opportunity to indicate length and strength when the opponents bid some suit you know they don't intend to play.

Avoid doubling an artificial bid without true strength in the suit. For example, you would not be too keen for your partner to lead a suit in which you held six to the jack. You double mainly with the idea that leading that suit for your side will develop tricks.

Responding to Partner's Overcall

Overcalls come in a variety of types, anchored by the simple overcall: they open the bidding, you bid something at a minimum level, as in 1 ♥—1 ♠. Or, they open the bidding, your partner passes, the next hand responds in some way, and you bid, as in 1 ♥—P—2 ♥—2 ♠. This, too, is a simple overcall.

Requirements for simple overcalls were covered earlier in this chapter. What was not discussed was your responsibilities as the partner of the overcaller, the "advancer" in bridge lingo. What should you do when your partner overcalls?

When your partner overcalls, the more of her trumps you hold, the more aggressive you can be in the bidding, especially if you have shortness in some other suit. If you can bid to a high level immediately in response to your partner's overcall, you rob the opponents of precious bidding space, and you have the protection of lots of trumps between the two hands.

Your action as advancer depends on your hand, and your choices are as follows:

- With no trump fit for your partner's suit, fewer than 10 HCP, and no good suit of your own to bid, pass.
- If you would have raised your partner's suit if he had opened the bidding instead of overcalling, do so directly unless third hand has bid and you will have to go to the three level to raise. Your raise to the two level does not promise much.
- If you have trump support and your hand evaluates to 10 or more support points, make a cuebid in opener's suit. That is, if opener started with 1 ♣ and partner overcalled 1 ♠, a bid of 2 ♣ by you tells partner that you have trump support and at least 10 support points.
- With at least four-card trump support and some shape—a singleton or void—and a weak hand, make a jump raise in partner's suit (for example, bid 3 ♠ if partner overcalled 1 ♠). You have a cuebid available to show a forward-going hand, so partner will not misunderstand your jump raise.
- With no fit for partner but with at least 10 HCP and a stopper in opener's suit, bid 1NT. On rare occasions, you will have enough to bid 2NT (12–14 HCP).

If your partner knows he can rely on you to raise with support after he overcalls, he won't bid his suit again after you pass unless he really has the goods.

A cuebid can be a bid in an opponent's suit, as in responding to an overcall. It can also be a direct bid over an opponent's opening bid. In that case, the cuebid shows a two-suited hand, almost always five cards in each of the suits. A cuebid can also be used in an uncontested auction to indicate "control" in the suit bid: that is, no more than one loser in the suit and often no quick losers (ace or void).

Balancing

In bridge, especially in duplicate bridge, the auction frequently turns into a skirmish between the two sides as they fight to win the contract. It is a losing strategy to go quietly, and it will behoove you to become familiar with a practice called balancing. In some countries, it's called "protection." No matter the name, the objective is the same: getting the opponents out of their comfort zone.

Suppose the bidding goes this way:

WEST	NORTH	EAST	SOUTH
		1 ♠	Pass
2 ♠	Pass	Pass	?

You are South and it's your turn to call. If you pass, the opponents get to play in 2 ♠. Is that okay with you? Your answer should be in the negative.

What can you do about this? First, consider what the relatively quiet auction has told you. Neither of your opponents seems to be loaded. West's 2 ♠ could be based on a mere 6 high-card points. If East had more than a minimum opener, she might have made some move toward game. It's logical to conclude that the high-card points are pretty evenly distributed between your side and theirs. You should make some move to get the opponents to a higher level. How you do that will depend on the makeup of your hand.

Suppose you hold:

♠ 32
♥ Q987
♦ KJ65
♣ K109

You didn't have enough strength to enter the fray directly over 1 ♠, but you should make a takeout double at this point. You may be thinking, "Wait!

I have only 9 high-card points!" That's true, but the auction strongly suggests that your partner has some of the missing strength. Think about it—the opponents are stopping in 2 ♠. If the opener has 12 or 13 high-card points and the responder has 6 or 7, that's about 20 high-card points in total. You have 9 high-card points, so your partner probably has 10 or 11 points.

That's what balancing is all about—inferring that your partner has a modicum of strength. By taking action, you are—in a very real sense—bidding your partner's cards as well as your own.

Here's another hand, same auction:

♠ 63
♥ 72
♦ KJ652
♣ KQ106

If you chose to balance at this point, what do you think is your best call? It might seem strange, but your proper bid is 2NT. You don't want to double because your hand will not be a good dummy if your partner bids 3 ♥. You could bid 3 ♦, but that will work out badly if your partner is short in that suit.

You can bid 1NT in the passout seat as an offer to play the contract, but any no-trump bid by a passed hand at the two level or higher will almost always show the minor suits with a lack of support for the other suits. Make sure you and your partner are in accord on this principle.

Involve your partner in the final decision by bidding 2NT, which can mean only that you have length in the minors—2NT cannot be an offer to play in no-trump at the two level. If you had that kind of hand, you would have overcalled 1NT at your first turn.

Discretion Rules

You don't always balance when the opponent stops at a low level. For example, you would pass if you held this hand in the passout seat (same auction):

♠ QJ109
♥ A3
♦ K652
♣ 843

The opponents have landed in your best suit. Why disturb them? Further, your holding in spades makes it clear your partner is short in spades, yet he took no action.

Another major factor in deciding whether to balance will be the vulnerability. If your side is vulnerable, you should be very leery of balancing when whatever you do (doubling or bidding) will require going to the three level (or making your partner do so). The opponents already know a lot about each other's hands and they will be quick to double you at the three level—and that can work out very badly, especially in duplicate. Balancing when vulnerable might be trading minus 110 (leaving the opponents to play in 2 ♠) for minus 200, 500, or worse.

You Open and They Compete

A vitally important principle of competitive bidding when your side has opened can, and probably should, be written in stone: support with support.

That is, when you have support for the partner's suit and enough strength to bid, let her know it as soon as possible. There's nothing worse than making an ambiguous bid, planning to support your partner's suit later, then finding that the bidding is in the stratosphere by the time it gets back to you.

By failing to show support, in many cases you will have deprived your partner of valuable information. You will be forced to guess what to do—never a good thing. It's a time-tested principle of competitive bidding that you always want to make the other person make the last guess.

When your partner opens the bidding, here are some basics for an accurate exchange of information. If your partner has opened one of a major and the next player bids a suit at the one level or two level:

- With 6–9 (or a "bad" 10) support points and at least three cards in partner's major, make a minimum raise, as in 1 ♥—1 ♠—2 ♥.
- With a "good" 10 or more support points, bid the overcaller's suit. This is known as a cuebid. It does not say you have overcaller's suit. It says you have trump support for partner but that your hand is too good to make a simple raise. You could even have an opening hand yourself, so even if partner tries to sign off below game, you will bid it yourself.
- Without support for partner but with 8–10 HCP and at least one stopper in opponent's suit bid at the one level, bid 1NT.
- Without support for partner and 11–12 HCP and at least one stopper in opponent's suit bid at the one level, bid 2NT.
- Without support for partner and 13–15 HCP and at least one stopper in the opponent's suit, bid 3NT.
- Without enough strength to bid at the two level, or without long suit to bid and no stopper in overcaller's suit, double for takeout (this is the "negative" double discussed earlier in this chapter).
- Without support for partner but with a good suit of your own and at least 10 HCP, bid your suit at a minimum level. Partner is not allowed to pass, so you should get more information about her hand when she takes another call.

The key in this situation is to act when you have some high-card values. Don't pass and hope to catch up later. That rarely works out well for your side.

Biting Your Tongue

There will be times when your partner opens the bidding and the next player bids a suit in which you are loaded. You will have visions of a four-digit number for your side after you double. If you and your partner have agreed to play negative doubles—and you should—you will have to pass. A double by you would be for takeout, not for penalty.

That sounds terribly frustrating, right? It would be if you haven't discussed all the nuances of playing negative doubles. When your partner opens the bidding and the next player bids, if you pass and the bidding comes back to your partner, she will look at her hand and, if short in the overcaller's suit, she will double as a way of "protecting" that big plus score you were hoping for.

You will, of course, happily pass your partner's "reopening" double, which ostensibly is for takeout. By passing, you will be converting it to the penalty double that you wanted to make directly.

Some hands will not be appropriate for a reopening double. If, for example, your partner opened a seven-card suit, she will be worried about how many tricks she will take in her long suit. If she has a second long suit, it might be better to bid that suit than to make a double. In such cases, if you were hoping to be able to penalize the opponents for a risky overcall, you can bid game in no-trump or in your partner's second suit if your hand is appropriate.

In the long run, you will benefit more from playing negative doubles than you will lose on occasion by not being able to exact heavy penalties.

CHAPTER 6

USEFUL BIDDING TOOLS
AND OTHER POINTERS

In the competitive bidding arena, communication and judgment are key elements of a successful game plan. You will not do well if you are timid in the bidding, but you must temper your aggression. Knowing when to pass is as important as knowing when to strike a blow.

Responding to a Takeout Double

There are two ways to get into the bidding when one of your opponents beats you to the punch with an opening bid—the overcall and the takeout double.

The parameters for takeout doubles were covered in the previous chapter, but it bears repeating that, with rare exceptions, the proper takeout double is roughly an opening hand with at least three-card support for any unbid suits.

The takeout double is not exclusively used in the direct seat after an opening bid. Third hand (the third player to bid after an opening) can also make a takeout double if the opener's suit is raised or if the responder bids a new suit. For example, if the opener started with 1 ♣ and the responder bids 1 ♥, a double by third hand shows support for diamonds and spades and roughly the equivalent of an opening hand.

There are two exceptions to the rule requiring support for unbid suits when a takeout double is made.

One is when you have a powerful hand (usually at least 17 high-card points) and a long, strong suit, something such as ♠ AKJ10976 or ♥ KQJ987.

The other is when you have a balanced hand with a stopper in the suit that was opened and more high-card points than it would show if you simply overcalled 1NT—19 or more high-card points when a 1NT overcall would be 15–18 points.

> When you make a takeout double and subsequently bid your own suit or no-trump, you are showing extra values. This is not a forcing bid—the responder can still pass with a truly bad hand but should strain to bid again, especially with support for the suit his partner has bid after doubling.

It is easy for the responder to the takeout double—sometimes known in bridge parlance as the "advancer"—to overlook this maneuver, and it might take a missed game or two for you and your partner to get used to this nuance. Just remember, making a takeout double and changing suits on your partner (or bidding no-trump) shows extra values—not simply that you doubled without support for unbid suits.

Tell Your Story

When your partner makes a takeout double of an opening bid and the next player passes, the spotlight is on you. You have one responsibility—to tell your partner what you've got. You should assume that your partner has a normal takeout double and respond accordingly.

Here are the guidelines for successful communication with your partner after he makes a takeout double:

- **With 0–8 HCP,** bid your best suit at a minimum level.
- **With 9–11 HCP,** make a jump bid in your best suit.
- **With a good 12 or more HCP,** start by cue-bidding the opponent's suit. This tells partner that your side belongs in game. The focus from that point usually will be to find a major-suit fit of at least eight

cards. If you do not uncover a fit in a major, attention will turn to no-trump.

- **With no good suit to bid but at least one stopper in the suit that was opened,** bid no-trump at the appropriate level: 1NT with 8–10 HCP, 2NT with 11–12 HCP, and 3NT with a good 13 HCP or more.

Suppose your partner doubles 1 ♣ for takeout and the next player passes. What is your action with the following hands?

♠ KQ3
♥ 62
♦ 10965
♣ 7632

Bid 1 ♦. True, you have no high-card points in that suit, but it would be poor strategy to bid a three-card spade suit in this case. Remember, your partner could have as few as three spades and still have a hand that qualifies for a takeout double.

♠ KQJ3
♥ 62
♦ 1096
♣ 7632

Bid 1 ♠. You have a good suit, but you are short of high-card points. Change the hand just a little, however, and you have a rosier view.

♠ KQJ3
♥ 62
♦ QJ65
♣ 763

Now your hand is too good for a simple 1 ♠ response. Think about it: you would bid 1 ♠ with zero high-card points and four spades to the 5. Your hand is much better than that. You must let your partner know when your hand is well above the minimum. Bid 2 ♠.

There is one occasion when you will make a cuebid without sufficient values to force to game. It's when your partner doubles a minor-suit opening and you have both majors. Here is an example:

♠ KQJ3
♥ QJ62
♦ Q9
♣ 763

This hand is good enough to make a jump bid to show invitational values, but which major should you choose? You could end up in a 4–3 fit if you guess wrong, but you don't have to guess. If your partner has doubled a 1 ♣ opener, simply bid 2 ♣. If your partner has only one major suit of at least four cards, he will bid it. If he has both, he will start with 2 ♥. You can then raise to 3 ♥ to show that your cuebid was based on an invitational hand. In considering whether to go on to game, he will use the information you have provided to help make that decision.

Be careful about cue-bidding without invitational values. If your hand falls short of the strength to invite game, simply bid the higher-ranking suit first, even if they are the same length.

> When you make a takeout double and your partner responds at a minimum level, it is prudent to assume her hand is at the bottom of the range for her bid. If the auction becomes competitive and your partner has another chance to speak, she can always take another bid if she is close to the maximum. Trust your partner to take action when appropriate.

There are many considerations beyond just high-card points in evaluating your hand after your partner has made a takeout double. For example, except for aces, honors you hold in the opener's suit should be discounted or at least devalued. Remember, your partner will tend to be short in the opener's suit when he makes a takeout double. If you think four to the queen in the opener's suit is worth anything, consider how many tricks you are likely to take in that suit if your partner puts a singleton 2 down in dummy.

When you are considering your bid in response to your partner's takeout double of a suit, you should envision your hand as providing support for one of your partner's suits. For example, when you hold six cards in a suit for which your partner has implied support, count two extra "support points" for the fifth and sixth cards. With that principle in mind, a hand with 8 high-card points and a six-card suit would count as 10. Make a jump bid to show your strength.

Improved Holdings

On the other hand, honors in suits that your partner has promised can be increased in value because they should be complementary. For example, you would not ordinarily assign much value to a doubleton queen. If your partner has promised that suit by way of a takeout double, you can look at that queen in a different light. It might still be worthless if your partner has only low cards in the suit, but it has potential at least.

The one card in the opener's suit that is good is the ace, especially facing shortness in your partner's hand. Having three or four to the ace opposite a singleton in dummy will give you the option of ruffing those low cards.

No Passing Fancy

When your partner makes a takeout double and you have a really dreadful hand, your natural inclination is to pass. Players are taught not to bid without values, right? Unfortunately, the worse your hand is, the more important it is to bid. If you have a poor hand and your partner has a minimum takeout double, you probably won't defeat their contract. That will annoy your partner and erode the trust between you. Just make the smallest "noise" you can and hope for the best.

> When you are faced with having to bid on a bad hand opposite a takeout double, don't let the opponents recognize your discomfort. Make your bid cheerfully and—outwardly, at least—without a care in the world. If the opponents sense you are in trouble, they are more likely to double when they have the balance of power. Bid with confidence.

There is one occasion on which you can pass your partner's takeout double—when you are loaded in the opener's suit. In that sense, you are selecting the opener's suit as trumps and converting the takeout double to a penalty double. In most cases, your partner will lead a trump if she has one, so your suit should be strong—something like **QJ10964**. Partner leads a trump because, just as when you are declarer, one of your first duties is to rake in the opponents' trumps so they can't be used for ruffing. You want to do the same to the declarer.

The Doubler's Second Call

When you have made a takeout double and your partner has responded, you will use the information you have gained from the response to decide what, if any, action to take next. There are two separate scenarios to consider after you have doubled and your partner has responded.

- Opener passes partner's response to your double.
- Opener bids again.

Consider this auction, with you as South:

WEST	NORTH	EAST	SOUTH
		1 ♣	Dbl
Pass	1 ♠	Pass	?

What does it mean if you now bid 2 ♠? First, consider that the partner's 1 ♠ bid shows 0–8 support points. If you bid 2 ♠, it should be an invitation to game in spades, asking your partner to bid 4 ♠ if she is close to the maximum for her bidding, typically 7 or 8 support points.

So, what should you have to bid 2 ♠? Well, if your partner is supposed to go to game with 7 support points, you need something along the lines of about 18 support points yourself. This is what a 2 ♠ bid in the given auction should look like:

♠ KQJ3
♥ AQJ6
♦ K1095
♣ 7

You have 16 good high-card points and a singleton. This is about a minimum for a free raise to 2 ♠.

What is a "free" bid or raise? A bid or raise is said to be "free" when it is made at a time when passing is an option. For example, if your partner opens 1 ♥ and the next player bids 1 ♠, you are under no obligation to bid—your partner will have another chance to call. If you bid another suit or raise your partner to 2 ♥, it is said to be free. Similarly, if your partner makes a takeout double and the next player bids or redoubles, you are off the hook. You do not have to respond, so any bid you make is said to be a "free" bid.

It's a different situation when there is competition. Going back to the auction in question:

WEST	NORTH	EAST	SOUTH
		1 ♣	Dbl
Pass	1 ♠	2 ♣	?

If you have four-card support for spades and a normal takeout double, it is important for you to bid 2 ♠ at this point. Why? If you don't, your partner will assume you don't have four spades and, holding only four herself, will probably sell out to the opponents even if she has a decent hand in the context of the bidding. She will not be that keen to play a 4–3 fit. If you suppress that four-card support, you will lose the part-score battle that is so important in bridge.

When the opponents have the boss suit—spades—the rules change slightly. If the opener rebids his suit after you make a takeout double and your partner has bid at a minimum level, you should have extra values to raise to the three level, even with four-card support. Your partner will keep that in mind if the bidding gets back to her. She will compete with an appropriate hand.

Heavy Lumber

The parameters for doubling and bidding a suit of your own have already been discussed, but a couple of examples are in order—along with an important principle.

Here are two hands good enough to double and then bid your own suit.

WEST	NORTH	EAST	SOUTH
		1 ♥	Dbl
Pass	2 ♦	Pass	?

♠ AKQJ76
♥ Q7
♦ AQJ
♣ 75

Bid 2 ♠, showing your strong hand and very good suit.

♠ AK4
♥ 75
♦ KJ
♣ AK10976

Bid 3 ♣. If your partner has a heart stopper and a smattering of points, he will probably bid 3NT. Remember, your bid of 3 ♣ is not forcing, and if your partner can't make a move over your strong bid, you probably don't want to be any higher.

Greater Efficiency

The reason you double with extra strength, planning to bid your own suit after your partner's response, is that the simple overcall has a very wide range, which hampers the bidding process to a degree.

When your hand is so strong that you need very little from your partner to make a game, your partner will frequently have what you need but be unable to move over a simple overcall. For example, suppose you hold:

♠ Q4
♥ 75
♦ K7653
♣ J1087

Your left-hand opponent opens 1 ♣. Your partner overcalls 1 ♠ and right-hand opponent passes. There's not much you can do. It's bad policy to raise your partner's simple overcall with a doubleton, and you certainly don't have enough to bid 1NT even though you do have a club stopper of sorts (a 1NT bid in this position shows a minimum of 9 or 10 high-card points and a stopper).

So you pass, as does the opener. Now suppose this is your partner's hand:

♠ AKJ1087
♥ 82
♦ AQ5
♣ A9

You have just missed a game that should have been bid. Clearly, your partner should have doubled first, then bid spades over your response of 2 ♦. You would happily raise to 3 ♠—you don't mind raising with a doubleton honor because, more often than not, your partner will have six spades—and you would soon be in 4 ♠.

Gotta Get to Game

Making a takeout double and later bidding your own suit shows strength, but it is not forcing when the responder to the double has bid at a minimum level. Any minimum bid could have been forced and the advancer might have zero high-card points.

When the advancer makes a bigger "noise" with his response—that is, jumps in a suit or bids no-trump—any new suit by the doubler is 100 percent forcing to game. The advancer must keep the bidding open, even if he cannot raise his partner's suit.

Discussing this with your partner will save a lot of headaches and teeth grinding over missed games. There are few things as frustrating as taking eleven or twelve tricks in a contract of 2 ♠.

Competing Against Preempts

In today's bridge world, the opponents are much more aggressive than in the early days of the game. That means you will occasionally find yourself faced with the problem of starting the bidding at the three level or higher.

Preemptive bidding is a two-edged sword, of course. Jumping around at high levels can cause your side more problems than you cause for the opponents, particularly when you open at a high level and find your partner with a good hand but no support for your suit. You will see when the dummy hits—your partner will pass most of the time—that your bid has kept the opponents out of trouble and landed you in a minus position.

Nevertheless, the pitfalls of aggressive preempting do not appreciably slow down some players, so you will have to learn ways of coping.

Fire versus Fire

An obvious tool is the takeout double, but some cautions are in order. The higher the preempt, the more you should have for a takeout double. What would qualify as a reasonable double of a 1 ♣ opener would fall woefully short of the requirements for a takeout double of 3 ♣, for example.

When the opponents possess the spade suit, even the three level is gone after an opener of 3 ♠ unless you or your partner can bid 3NT.

When an opponent starts the bidding at the two level or higher, especially in first seat, you risk going for a number if you bid or double. Why does the first-seat preempt make a difference? Mainly because nothing is known about the other two hands. The next player could be loaded and ready to double you. On the other hand, if you pass, it could be your partner with the goods, so going quietly could result in your missing game.

With that in mind, it is best to be consistent in your approach. If you generally have a conservative style—you don't bid on marginal hands—your partner will take that into account if the opening preemptive bid comes to him after two passes. Similarly, if you normally take an aggressive stance, your partner will know you probably don't have much if you pass. This will help your partner make more accurate guesses in close situations.

Minimum Standards

Do not let emotion dictate your action. Yes, it is annoying to have an opponent start with 2 ♠ against you. If you let that get under your skin and you bid just to show them they can't push you around, your results will suffer in the long run. Your partner should have confidence in your bidding.

It's difficult to outline specific guidelines because preemptive bidding takes many forms, and the methods available will vary from pair to pair. In general, it will probably pay to be slightly aggressive in combating preemptive bids, especially when the vulnerability is favorable (they are, you aren't). Vulnerable overcalls should be sound and based on good suits, and you should be very sound when the vulnerability is unfavorable (you are, they aren't).

The level at which you have to bid also makes a difference. You can be a bit friskier if you can get in there at the two level, as when the opponents open with a weak 2 ♦ or when your partner might be able to bid at the two level over your takeout double.

The Rule of Eight

A handy tool for helping you get into the bidding over weak two-bids is known as the Rule of Eight.

Here's how it works. When your right-hand opponent opens with a weak two-bid, assume that your partner will have, on average, about 8 high-card points scattered through his hand. If you think that your partner's 8 high-card points will be enough for you to have a shot at whatever you are considering bidding, go ahead and take the plunge. If you need substantially more help than the average hand your partner will provide for you, look again at your thirteen cards and reconsider your decision to get involved.

> If you and your partner are in accord about the use of the Rule of Eight, be sure to apply it when it is your turn to bid after your partner overcalls. When your partner bids over a two-level opener, be aware that he is counting on you for about 8 high-card points. If that's all you have, it's best not to raise your partner's bid, even with trump support. If you have good trumps and 9 or 10 support points, you can raise.

The Rule of Eight has other applications. Say the dealer opens a weak 2 ♥. If you now bid 3 ♣, that is a strong bid, not a weak one. You don't preempt over preempts. Just as with a two-level bid, the overcaller is counting on her partner for about 8 support points. The difference is that when the overcaller bids 3 ♠ instead of 2 ♠, she is saying to her partner, "I'm counting on you for 8 support points. If you have them, put me in game if we have a fit in spades—or do something else intelligent. If you don't have the points or we don't have a good spade fit, pass."

The Rule of Eight loses its effectiveness when the opponents are opening the bidding at the three level and higher, so be a bit more careful when you have to start at higher levels.

Suit Quality

When you overcall at the two level or higher, it generally shows at least good suit. You are not always blessed with extra length or good intermediate cards in a hand that cries out for some action. For example, say an opponent opens 2 ♥ in front of you and you hold this hand:

♠ K7654
♥ 82
♦ A3
♣ AK109

You have a ratty spade suit, but you have a good hand with prime cards (aces and kings). You can't overcall in no-trump because you don't have hearts stopped and you don't have the high-card strength anyway. A takeout double is out because you can't support diamonds and if you bid 3 ♠ over 3 ♦, it shows a much stronger hand than you have (not to mention a much stronger suit). Passing is a very wimpy action. Yes, you could get nailed if the opener's partner has a big spade stack behind you and some high-card points, but your partner could also have those spades and points, so passing might let the opponents steal your game from you.

You might be a bit uncomfortable bidding 2 ♠ with this hand, but you have to do it.

Compensation

Be sure, however, that you have compensating values if your suit is not of the best quality or length. Translation: it's okay to overcall a somewhat ratty suit if your hand is pretty good and passing doesn't feel like a reasonable option.

The bottom line is that when the opponents are taking up your bidding space, you will have to make some compromises.

Cuebids

We've mentioned this tool before, but now we'll discuss it in more detail. The cuebid takes many forms in bridge, making it a valuable tool in your bidding arsenal. To many players, the various cuebids are essential to survival in the competitive bidding arena.

One of the most popular and easiest to use is the Michaels cuebid, named for its inventor, Mike Michaels.

In the old days, if someone opened one of a suit and the next player bid two of the same suit (as in 1 ♣—2 ♣) that showed a very strong hand and directed his partner to pick his best suit. It was more or less a takeout double on steroids.

Hands that qualified for the super-strong takeout were few and far between, however, so Michaels devised a better use for the direct cuebid. Here it is:

- **Over one of a minor,** the bid of the same minor shows at least five cards in each major in a hand that is either somewhat weak or very strong. When the hand is very strong, the Michaels bidder is just waiting to see which major his partner likes better so that he can make a strong game invitation or a raise to game in that suit.
- **Over one of a major,** a bid of the same major shows at least five cards in the other major and at least five cards in either minor. When advancer doesn't fit partner's major, he bids 3 ♣ to tell partner, "Pass if this is your minor suit—or correct to diamonds."

The Michaels cuebid is a handy convention that comes up more often than you might think, and it's great when you uncover that big trump fit. You can blow the opponents out of the water by jacking up the bidding in a hurry. It's not so great when you don't have a good fit in one of the Michaels bidder's two suits. Furthermore, if the other side ends up playing the contract, the information provided by the cuebid will help the declarer play as though she can see all the cards.

Still, few duplicate players would consider playing without Michaels.

Info, Please

Another vital use for the cuebid in competition occurs when the other side opens the bidding and your side overcalls. You will always raise your partner's overcall when possible, but it's best, considering how light the overcaller might be, not to have to make a jump raise to show a raise with a bit extra.

That's where the cuebid comes in. Consider this auction (you are South):

WEST	NORTH	EAST	SOUTH
1 ♥	1 ♠	Pass	?

Now suppose you hold this hand:

♠ KJ65
♥ 82
♦ AQ3
♣ 7654

You will certainly raise your partner's overcall, but if you bid just 2 ♠, your partner will pass with this hand:

♠ AQ1098
♥ KQ3
♦ J1087
♣ 2

As you can see, game is almost certain, but North will never make a move toward game over a simple raise, which could be based on as little as 6 high-card points.

Of course, if you have to jump to 3 ♠ to show your good support—akin to a limit raise of an opening bid—you might catch your partner with this hand:

♠ AQ1098
♥ K3
♦ 654
♣ 983

A 1 ♠ overcall is perfectly reasonable with that hand, but the partnership is now too high. You can avoid this kind of problem when you have a limit-raise type of hand (or better) by cuebidding to show it. If your partner thinks game might be in the offing over a limit raise, she can make a game try in one of her suits. If she signs off to show no game interest opposite a limit raise, you have succeeded in staying at a safe level.

Getting to No-Trump

You have seen the cuebid in use when your partner makes a takeout double and you have a good hand. You show it by bidding the opener's suit.

When you and your partner have found a big fit in a minor and think you have enough for game, you usually prefer to play in 3NT, which scores better in a duplicate game and also requires two fewer tricks than 5 ♣ or 5 ♦.

One way to get there is to use the cuebid to ask your partner for a stopper in the opener's suit.

Here is a typical auction (you are South):

WEST	NORTH	EAST	SOUTH
1 ♥	2 ♣	Pass	2 ♥
Pass	3 ♥	Pass	3NT
All Pass			

The first cuebid (yours) says you have a fine hand in support of clubs. Partner makes a second cuebid to say, "If you can stop hearts, we can probably take nine tricks in 3NT."

Your hand might be:

♠ AJ10
♥ K103
♦ QJ10
♣ Q873

Partner could have something like:

♠ K54
♥ 6
♦ K65
♣ AK10965

You will make 3NT with ease on the combined hands.

In the Balancing Seat

Balancing—taking some action when passing will end the auction—was covered in an earlier chapter, but only in routine auctions, such as when an opening bid of one of a suit is followed by two passes or when the opponents bid and raise a suit and opt to bid no higher. It is established that it can be beneficial to try to push them one level higher with some kind of action.

When the opening bid is at the two level or higher and the next two players pass, the person in the passout seat will have objectives that differ vastly from the typical balancing decision.

The fact that the opening bidder has started the auction so much higher means that if you bid, you may have to do so at a level that is not justified by the cards you hold. Yes, as in other balancing situations, you will be bidding your partner's cards as well as your own, but even if your partner has more than you have a right to expect, it might still not be enough.

Also, when balancing over a preempt, you are not trying to push the opponents to a higher level. You are trying to claim what is yours. In many of these cases, it's your hand. You just have to figure out where to play it.

No Bid, No Fit

In these days of aggressive bidding, it is normal for the partner of the preemptive bidder to increase the preemption when he has support for the opener's suit. There is a measure of safety when your side has an abundance of trumps, and most astute players take advantage of that, especially when not vulnerable, and even more so when the opponents are.

What that means for you in the balancing seat is that if the bidding goes 2 ♥—P—P, there is a fair likelihood that your right-hand opponent does not have a fit for the opening bidder. That might or might not be a danger sign. Just because the opener's partner lacks a fit does not mean he is loaded and just waiting for you to take some action so that he can pounce on you with a penalty double. He could simply have a weak hand. If that is the case, however, why didn't your partner do something?

Here are possible explanations for your partner's failure to act over the preempt:

- Partner has a poor hand that does not justify taking action.
- Partner has a good hand but does not have a long suit to bid and does not have a stopper in opener's suit and cannot make a takeout double because he cannot stand for you to bid a particular suit.
- Partner has a good hand and a hefty holding in opener's suit and is hoping you will balance with a double so that he can convert it to penalty by passing and thereby collect a big number.

You must consider all of these possibilities when you find yourself in the balancing seat after an opening preempt has been followed by two passes.

> If you find a partner who is disciplined enough to pass a good hand over a preempt when she has no good action, sign her to a long-term contract if you can. She is a winning player, in contrast to those who have been heard to say after a bidding disaster, "But I had to bid—I had 14 points."

Being short in the opener's suit is the first hint that a double might work out best for your side. Be careful, however, about doubling just because you have only one or two cards in the opener's suit. If your hand is weak, your partner's trump tricks may be the only tricks for your side. To double in the balancing seat when your partner might pass for penalty, you should have a minimum of two quick tricks.

Dummy Quality

Second, consider whether you will be happy about putting your hand down as the dummy should your partner bid in response to your double. Sometimes your partner will have length in the opener's suit without good spots and will decide to bid even when she has a few of the opener's trumps. Sometimes your partner has no semblance of a trump trick and simply has to bid. She won't be happy to find a doubleton in the suit she selects.

Of course, there will be many occasions when your course of action in the passout seat will be clear-cut. Perhaps you will have a long, strong suit to bid. You might have the equivalent of a 1NT opener (with a stopper in the opener's suit). You can show that by bidding 2NT in the balancing seat. You might have a classic takeout double with a bit extra to compensate for the higher level of the bidding.

The bottom line, however, is that those nasty preempts will make your life miserable when you don't have any easy decision in fourth seat. As with other competitive decisions, you will be well served to try to be consistent in your courses of action, and disciplined enough to pass when you know it's right. You will not win every battle with a preempt—that's why players throw them at you—but you will profit in the long run with a sound, disciplined approach.

PART 3

THE PLAY OF
THE HAND

CHAPTER 7

DECLARER'S PRIORITIES

You have to win tricks when you play the hand. You will develop cunning, guile, and deception. Some situations require that you win tricks immediately. Other hands will require that you lose tricks when it serves your purpose. You command twenty-six warriors and play them in concert to defeat your opponents. Compared to bridge, any other card game is like playing tennis with the net down.

Card Play

In the following situations you are going to be the declarer. The cards will be listed as being in your hand or in dummy. You have to figure out how many tricks you are going to win. In this beginning exercise, neither the suit nor the contract matters.

In each case, you will be determining how many tricks you can win. Since the rules of bridge require that you lead from the hand that won the last trick, the situation will be set, giving you the lead from hand or from dummy. There will be a progression of examples that will develop your ability to take tricks.

You will, of course, have thirteen cards in your hand when you start to play in an actual game, but for the next few exercises we'll concentrate on one suit.

Counting Winners

Count the winners for this suit between you and your partner.

```
DUMMY
AK

DECLARER
(VOID)
```

If you are leading from your hand, you have no cards in this suit to lead to your winning ace and king in dummy. If you are leading from dummy, you will be able to play both high cards. You will have to discard two cards in your hand from another suit.

> When a suit is led and you are void in that suit, you may discard any card you choose. In a trump contract, you may use a trump card to win the trick, or you may discard. Discards are valuable in trump contracts. They are not as valuable in no-trump contracts.

Spotting Entries

Add just one card to your hand and you have an entry to the ace and king in dummy.

```
DUMMY
AK

DECLARER
2
```

That is, you can lead the 2 to gain entry to the dummy's ace and king. Now, no matter what, you will win two tricks. If you are leading from your hand, you lead the 2 and win that trick and the next with your two winners. You have used the 2 to "get to" the dummy. When you play the king from dummy, you must discard from your hand.

> When you lead a losing card toward a winning card, you have gained entry to the hand containing the winning card. It is a means of securing the lead in the hand of your choice. "Transportation," in bridge terminology, is the ability to get from one hand to the other.

Guess how many tricks this combination of cards will win? No matter what, you will win two tricks. If you are leading from your hand you have transportation. You have two entries to the dummy if you so choose (win the first trick in dummy with the queen and the next one with the ace). You may also use the king in your hand to overtake the queen if you want to be in your hand. When you plan well, you can have an entry to either hand, and you can win the second trick in whichever hand you choose.

```
DUMMY
AQ

DECLARER
KJ
```

The idea of transportation in bridge is fascinating. Getting from your hand to the dummy and back is what transportation is all about. It is about deciding where to win a trick when you have a choice.

Using Entries—Transportation

These are the cards of the same suit (the type of suit doesn't matter) between you and your partner:

```
DUMMY
KQ3

DECLARER
AJ
```

In this example you have a choice. You have two entries to your hand or you can win three tricks ending in dummy. The only way you can win three tricks is to play the ace first and play the 3 from dummy. Next you would lead the jack and win with the king or queen. The other high card would win the third trick. You will win three tricks, and you will have one discard.

```
DUMMY
KQ43

DECLARER
AJ
```

Now, try this situation. No matter how you play it out, you will win only three tricks at the very most (assuming no cards in this suit have been discarded by the opponents before you start playing it). If you do not play carefully, you will win only two tricks. Because you have so many face cards in the suit, it could be easy to mess this up. If you play the jack from your hand first, it will win because there are no higher cards in the suit held by the opponents. Unfortunately for you, none of the cards in dummy would then be higher than the only card left in that suit in your hand—the ace. In bridge parlance, you have "blocked" the suit.

In the given example, if you led the ace on the first trick, you would then lead the jack from your hand and overtake for the second trick. The third high card, or honor, would then win the third trick. You would then have only a low card in dummy remaining. That low card probably wouldn't take a trick. You will win three tricks, and you will have one discard in your hand.

Unblocking and Counting Cards

Get a deck of cards and sort out these cards and set them up exactly the way they are set in the following box.

```
DUMMY
♠ KQJ54

DECLARER
♠ A3
```

No matter which hand leads, you must win the first trick with the ace. This technique unblocks the suit and allows you to win the remaining tricks in dummy. Next you will lead the 3 and win the second trick in dummy with the king, the third trick with the queen, and so on. If both opponents follow suit to the first two leads of this suit, all the cards in that suit will be good.

Let's back up a bit. You will now start to count the cards played. It's easy.

- Trick #1—Play the ♠ A from your hand and the ♠ 4 from dummy. The opponents each play a spade to the trick. Four spades have been played.
- Trick #2—You lead the ♠ 3 from your hand and win with the king in dummy.

Each opponent plays a spade. So now eight of them have been played. You have three cards remaining in dummy. That totals eleven cards. The opponents have two cards remaining between them. You have the Q J5 remaining in dummy to win the last three tricks.

That ♠ 5 becomes a winner because it is the only one left in the suit. You have established the ♠ 5 as a winning card. Between your hand and the dummy, you held seven of the thirteen cards in the suit. As long as one opponent held two cards in the suit, you win five tricks.

Unblocking and Using an Entry

This example will have two suits.

DUMMY		DECLARER	
♠	♥	♠	♥
K	A	A	9
Q			8
J			7
10			6
9			5
8			4
7			3

The example is set up vertically to get you used to viewing the cards from the correct perspective. When you are declaring, you see the cards in vertical columns.

The declarer has eight cards, as does the dummy. You are going to play these cards to win all eight tricks. How will you do that? If you play any heart card from your hand first, you will only win two tricks. The first trick you win will be the ♥ A in dummy. You will then have to lead a spade from dummy and win with the ♠ A in your hand. You will have to lead a heart, and the opponents will win the next six tricks.

Now, look at what happens if you unblock the spades first by playing the ♠ A. It wins the trick, and you are still in your hand. Next you lead a low heart and win it in dummy with the ace. Now you can lead all those good spades from the top down, winning each and every trick and discarding a heart on each of those tricks. You win eight tricks.

> The point is to win with high cards in the short hand. If a six-card suit is divided with four cards in your hand and two in dummy, then the dummy is the short hand. Short suits in dummy are valuable when you are playing in a trump contract.

In review, you won the ♠ A and then led a heart to the dummy, winning with the ♥ A, and then you led the spades, winning six more tricks.

Creating an Entry with Trump

Look at this set of cards. You will play the same cards in two different contracts. The first contract will be 7NT, the second 7 ♠. You are playing this hand in 7NT and you are not happy. Look at what happens. Your left-hand opponent leads the ♣ Q. You win with the ace. You can win the ♣ K, the ♦ A, and ♦ K, the ♥ A, and the ♠ A for a grand total of six tricks. Alas, you have no way to get to the dummy. All those luscious spades are going to waste.

Let's try again. This time you will be playing in 7 ♠. The opponent leads the ♣ Q again, and

```
DUMMY
♠ KQJ109872
♥ 6
♦ 432
♣ 4

DECLARER
♠ A
♥ A108764
♦ AK76
♣ AK
```

you win with the ♣ A. You win the second trick with the ♠ A. Playing the high card from the short side in spades unblocks the suit. Next you play the ♥ A, winning the trick. Now you play a low heart from your hand. You have no hearts in dummy, so you can ruff with the ♠ 7. The term "ruff" means using your trump cards to win tricks. You have used the trump suit as transportation to the dummy.

Now you will win eight tricks in spades, one in hearts, two in diamonds, and two in clubs for a total of thirteen. Much more satisfying, no?

Trump Suit Distribution

Spades are the trump suit:

```
DUMMY
♠ AKQJ10987

DECLARER
♠ 6
```

When the spade suit is led you will win with the ♠ A and then play them from the top, winning eight tricks. You have a nine-card fit. Since you hold nine cards in the trump suit, your opponents have four. How many times would you have to lead this suit to pull the opponents' fangs? That is, how many times do you have to lead the suit to get all their trumps away from them—and that is something you want to do because the opponents' trumps are potential winners for them. If you leave them outstanding and start playing your plain suits (non-trump suits), the opponents will be ruffing your winners.

The "distribution" of a suit is the number of cards of the specific suit in each of the four hands. First establish the number of outstanding cards. Do that by adding the number of cards you can see and subtracting that number from thirteen. For example, when you can see nine cards, the outstanding number is four.

How many rounds it takes to pull the opponents' trumps depends on how they divide. If the four trumps in the opponents' hands are divided 2–2, it will take two rounds to reel them all in. If they split 3–1 (more likely, according to the odds), you'll have to play three rounds.

If you lead the suit once and one opponent does not follow suit, then the four outstanding cards are distributed with zero cards in one hand and four in the other. You now know there are three outstanding trumps and they are all in one hand. If you lead the suit and both opponents follow, then you know there are two outstanding trumps left (split evenly or sitting in one of the opponents' hands).

If you lead the suit twice and both opponents follow suit, then you know the suit has been cleared and you alone hold the remaining trump. You have pulled the trumps and cleared the suit.

> When you have played a suit enough times to know that there are no more cards in the suit remaining in the opponents' hands, then the suit is cleared and you have all the remaining cards in the suit. A major goal when playing in trump is to pull trumps until you clear the suit. In no-trump, a major goal is to clear your long suit so as to make your low cards winners.

In the next hand you also have the top-nine spades, but the distribution of the suit is different.

```
DUMMY
♠ AKQJ

DECLARER
♠ 109876
```

How many tricks can you win in this suit? If you do not have an entry to your hand in another suit, you will win only four tricks. The last spade will be in your hand, but the lead will be in dummy. You will have no transportation in this suit. Every time a spade is led, it will be won in dummy. You have four entries to the dummy, but if spades are trump, then you will win at least five tricks.

```
DUMMY
♥ AKQJ87

DECLARER
♥ 109
```

You will win six tricks, and look—you actually have an entry to your hand. If you play the ♥ 7 or the ♥ 8 first, you can win with the ♥ 9 in your hand and then lead back to the dummy to take the remaining tricks. You have one entry to your hand and two entries to the dummy. You will win six tricks in this suit. How many trumps are outstanding? You have eight; the opponents have five. Again, they can be distributed only three ways. Let's list the distributions the way you should start to think about them: 5–0, 4–1, or 3–2. That means trumps can be five in one hand, none in the other, and so forth. If you get your mind around these numbers, they will become second nature to you and will help you with one of the most important chores you must master to become a good player—the ability to count.

Delayed Winners and Counting Losers

At times you cannot win a trick immediately. This is true whenever the opponents hold the ace of the suit. You need to find a way to get rid of your losers. First, learn to identify a loser in bridge.

```
┌─────────────────────────┐
│  DUMMY                   │
│  KQ                      │
│                          │
│  DECLARER                │
│  J10                     │
└─────────────────────────┘
```

You have one loser. After the opponents play the ace, you have one winner. How many tricks can you win with this holding? Only one. You will win a trick with this suit if an opponent declines to play the ace on the trick, but in most cases you will win a trick after the ace has been played. At that point, you have one winner. The winner is not a quick trick, but it is a delayed winner. This holding has one loser, one eventual winner, one entry to your hand, and no discards. Add just one card, and see what happens:

```
┌─────────────────────────┐
│  DUMMY                   │
│  KQ4                     │
│                          │
│  DECLARER                │
│  J10                     │
└─────────────────────────┘
```

This holding contains one loser, two eventual winners, one entry to the dummy, and one discard in your hand. That little 4 is mighty. Its presence gives you another eventual winner, and a discard in your hand.

```
┌─────────────────────────┐
│  DUMMY                   │
│  K                       │
│                          │
│  DECLARER                │
│  9643                    │
└─────────────────────────┘
```

The story on this holding is ugly. You have four losers, no eventual winners, no entries, and no discards. Even worse, the king is sitting there by itself in dummy. Both opponents can see it, so there's no way you could sneak past the ace, as you might do if the singleton king were in your hand.

```
DUMMY

QJ3

DECLARER

1094
```

No matter what, you will win one trick with this holding. When the opponents play the ace and king, you will have the queen remaining to win a trick. If you lead the suit, or if the opponents lead the suit, you will always win one trick. You have the Q J109 split between the two hands. All these cards are equal.

```
DUMMY

Q85

DECLARER

J2
```

"Touching cards" are any number of cards that are next to one another in rank. The ace and king are touching cards, as are the 7 and 6. So, if you have the AKQJ10 in one hand, they are equal in value.

If you lead this suit, you can be sure of winning a trick only if the ace and king are on your left. If the opponents lead the suit, you will always get a trick. If a low card is led from either side of the table, simply play low. Your right-hand opponent wins with the king and returns another card in this suit. You must play the jack from your hand. Lefty wins with the ace and plays another card in this suit; your queen will win on the board (another name for the dummy). If you lead the suit, you won't win a trick unless your left-hand opponent has both high honors. If the honors are split, you cannot win a trick if you lead this suit yourself.

> When you play a card higher than the one that has been played, you have "covered." You cover when you play a card just high enough to beat the prevailing high card. When you do not play a card higher, you have "ducked"; that is, you have played a low card.

You have learned the basic principles for counting and winning tricks. This knowledge will serve you well at trump or no-trump contracts. There is a basic difference between the two types of contracts. In a trump contract you can use trumps to win tricks and provide entries when you become void in a suit. In no-trump contracts, you do not have the safety net of trumps, so your goal will be to develop tricks in suits that hold promise for promotion.

To this point, this chapter has only covered playing cards that are touching, or in sequence. In actual play, though, you will find that you have combinations of honor cards that are broken up with one or two intervening cards missing. The play that you are about to learn is called a "finesse." Here is how it works.

```
DUMMY
AQ

DECLARER
32
```

If you are playing from your hand, you lead a card toward the dummy. You see that you do not have the king in this suit. You can certainly win one trick by playing the ace first. The queen will then lose to the king unless the king falls under the ace (very unlikely when you have only four cards in the suit). There's a better plan for winning two cards in this suit.

Lead the 2 from your hand, and if your left-hand opponent does not play the king, you will play the queen from dummy and see what happens. It may win the trick. In fact, it will win the trick if your left-hand opponent has the king and did not play it. In that case, you have finessed against the king and won two tricks.

If your left-hand opponent did have the king and played it on the first trick (a silly thing to do, usually), you will cover the king with the ace, winning the trick. The queen is then the highest-ranking card remaining and she will win a trick whenever she is played.

Also notice that if the king is on your right, you won't win two tricks unless your right-hand opponent is asleep or trying very hard to win your favor. The queen will always lose to the king but you have given yourself an extra chance to win a trick. A finesse is meant to maximize your odds.

A mystery unfolds for your partner when you lead the fourth-best card in your longest suit. With a simple application of arithmetic your partner will immediately know a lot about the distribution of the suit and who has what. The tool she is using is known as the Rule of Eleven. Your partner considers the value of the card you led, say the ♥ 5. That number is subtracted from 11. Your partner now knows there are six cards higher than your 5 in the other three hands, and she can now see her own hand and the dummy to figure out how many cards higher than the 5 are in the declarer's hand. This can be useful as the play progresses.

CHAPTER 8

WHEN YOU'RE ON DEFENSE

Up to now we've been discussing your play if you and your partner have won the auction. But what happens when your opponents win it? Now your objective, rather than to fill the contract, becomes preventing them from filling theirs.

The fact that the defenders have the first shot is an advantage to them, a good thing—at least from the defenders' point of view—because the declarer has the advantage of being able to see all the assets between his hand and the dummy.

Defenders, of course, can also see the dummy, but in general they are not as aware of their combined strengths as the declarer is of his. As a defender, you have a target of the number of tricks you are trying to take. If the declarer is in a game contract in a major, he must take ten tricks. Your goal as a defender is to get four tricks, leaving him at least one short.

If the contract is 3 ♦, you and your partner must do your best to take five tricks. It pays to keep your goal in mind at all times. In a sense, it's a race. In 3 ♦, for example, the declarer is trying to get nine tricks before you and your partner get five. First one to his or her goal is the winner.

Listening to the Auction

The language of bidding is meant to convey information. That's how partners find out their best contract and how high they should go in the auction. At the same time, the opponents are listening—or they should be—and they are privy to the same information. On many occasions, they can use that information to ferret out the best opening lead, best meaning the most damaging to the declarer.

One of the most common ways that "listening to the auction" can help you is when the declarer has bid two suits and his partner has preferred the first one. Here's an example:

WEST	NORTH	EAST	SOUTH
			1 ♠
Pass	1NT	Pass	2 ♥
Pass	2 ♠	All Pass	

Suppose this is your hand:

♠ 43
♥ KJ109
♦ J1098
♣ K54

Normally, that ♦ J stands out as the opening lead because you have such a good sequence. You dream of finding the king in dummy and your partner with the ace and queen. You might start off with the first three tricks.

Cut Down the Ruffs

That heart suit is also tough-looking, and your right-hand opponent, the declarer, has announced that she has at least four of them. You have the declarer's second suit under control for sure, but let's look at what you know about the dummy.

For starters, North (the dummy) bid 1NT after his partner opened 1 ♠. That means the dummy probably has no more than two spades. If he had more, he would have raised spades. When South showed her second suit, the dummy went back to the first one. There's a good chance the dummy will have a doubleton heart to go with the doubleton spade. The dummy's hand could easily be:

♠ J5
♥ 86
♦ AK432
♣ 8752

If you start with the ♦ J, the declarer will win with the ace and play a heart to the ace and another heart. If you don't play a trump right away, there's a good chance the declarer will get to ruff both of her heart losers in dummy.

Do you see where this is going? You have strength in the declarer's second suit and you have a means of keeping her from getting rid of those losers by ruffing them. If you start with a trump, you can win the second round of hearts and play another trump, eliminating spades from the dummy and keeping the declarer from using them to ruff hearts. This might or might not defeat the contract, but it will certainly save at least one trick.

Here's a good "listening to the auction" case to study:

WEST	NORTH	EAST	SOUTH
			1 ♠
Pass	2 ♦	Pass	2 ♠
Pass	4 ♠	Pass	4NT
Pass	5 ♦	Pass	6 ♠
All Pass			

You are West. Your hand is:

♠ 98
♥ K8732
♦ A6
♣ 10986

The opponents have had a strong auction to the small slam. They need twelve tricks to make their contract. What do you know about the entire deal?

You know that North's bidding shows spade support and a good diamond suit—in bridge parlance, the diamond suit is a "source of tricks." Now, you know the diamond suit is not running yet because you have the ace. So what can you do about it? What's your plan?

Get Yours First

You know that if you start out passively, the declarer will pull trumps and start working on the diamonds, which will eventually produce four or five tricks. There's probably not much you can do about the establishment of the diamond suit, so you must try to build a trick for your side before the declarer has a chance to go after the diamonds.

Are you closer to making your decision about your opening lead? You should be. Ask yourself: what is our best chance for developing a trick for our side before the declarer starts working on the diamonds?

A club could work out, but the declarer didn't get excited until he heard about his partner's great diamonds and trump support, then he launched into Blackwood and sailed into the slam. He is probably pretty well heeled in clubs. The declarer almost surely has the ♥ A—he wouldn't bid Blackwood with two or more quick losers in the suit—and is counting on the dummy to have an entry to diamonds once they're set up. That puts the ♣ A in dummy, so the declarer almost surely has a strong holding in that suit. Even if your partner has the queen and jack of clubs, you don't have "time" to get that suit going. The declarer will be drawing trumps and playing on diamonds any second now.

That leaves you with only one choice: a heart. Oh, but what if you lead right into the ♥ AQ in your partner's hand? You are still virtually certain to take your ♦ A anyway, and you will have taken your best shot at building a trick for your side. Leading into the ♥ AQ is not likely to be the difference maker. It would mean only that the slam was unbeatable.

What you are hoping for is that your partner has the ♥ Q so that the declarer will have to play his ace, leaving him at least one loser in hearts when you come in with your ♦ A. You hope the entire deal looks like this:

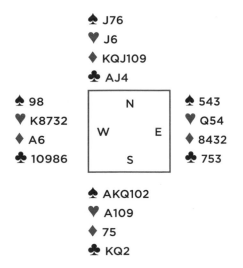

You can see the devastating effect of your heart lead. Your partner will play the queen, knocking out the ace. When the declarer plays on diamonds—he has no choice and can do no more than hope for a miracle or a huge mistake by you—you will win the ace and cash your ♥ K.

What happens without a heart lead? The declarer wins, pulls trumps, and plays a diamond. After you take your ace, the declarer will have three discards coming—remember, he has only two diamonds and the dummy has five really luscious ones. Those diamonds will be used to get rid of the ♥ 109. He won't even need the third discard because his hand will be high and he will make the slam.

Opening Leads on Defense

The opponents won the contract; it happens. Get the defense off to a good start. That is your goal when you are playing defense. The opening lead is the first salvo in the battle to win tricks. As you first start playing bridge, you will think that leading winning cards on defense is the best way. Unfortunately, it is not a good tactic against no-trump contracts unless you have both the ace and king of a suit and some lower cards to back up those honors.

Opening Leads Against No-Trump Contracts

First, let's consider what you want to do in an uncontested auction. That is an auction when you and your partner have only passed. A typical auction would be:

WEST	NORTH	EAST	SOUTH
		1NT	Pass
3NT	Pass	Pass	Pass

You know East has 15–17 high-card points, and West has about 10, maybe a few more. For the purpose of playing defense with this type of auction, figure that the opener has 16 high-card points and that the responder has 10. Your first consideration will be to calculate how many high-card points are remaining for your partner to hold.

♠ K10764
♥ 32
♦ K9764
♣ 8

Your partner has about 8 high-card points. You know this because you add the number of known high-card points in each of the hands. The opponents have a combined 26 high-card points, you have 6, and the remaining high-card points are in your partner's hand. It's only simple arithmetic and you can do it.

> When firing the opening salvo against a no-trump contract, lead the fourth-highest card from your longest suit. Although not a high card, it's an aggressive lead. Your goal is to win control of the suit led by retaining high cards in that suit. The logic is that you're trying to retain your high cards for later. When you lead your fourth-highest card, your partner will know your best suit.

In this type of auction, it is usually best to lead from your longest suit. You will consider two questions. First, what suit, and second, which card? A general rule when leading against a no-trump contract is to lead your fourth-best card from your longest suit. With this hand, you have two five-card suits, both spades and diamonds. Which one to choose?

Neither of the opponents has bid a major suit. West has not used the Stayman convention asking the 1NT opener for a major suit. The suggestion is that the opponents are weak in one of the two major suits. The only hope from your perspective is that the opponents' weakness is in spades. You will lead the fourth-highest card from your spade suit, specifically, the ♠ 6.

♠ 83
♥ Q1084
♦ Q1084
♣ J76

With this hand, you hold 5 high-card points, and your partner should have about 9. Your only information from the auction is that your opponents have not tried to find a game contract in a major suit by using the Stayman convention. Your best bet is to lead the fourth-highest card from your major suit. Specifically, lead the ♥ 4.

Here is your hand:

♠ 5
♥ QJ104
♦ K1052
♣ AK43

Your partner has very few points. You can do the arithmetic and give your partner about 1 high-card point, maybe none at all. You will probably have to win all the tricks for your side. To figure out what you want to lead, first consider which suit you do not want to lead.

You do not want to lead a singleton against no-trump. You can eliminate the spade suit from consideration. Your club holding is very nice and will win two tricks. Save those for later and eliminate that suit from consideration. You are left with hearts or diamonds.

If you lead a diamond you would have to force out the ace, queen, and jack to win an extra trick. On the other hand, if the declarer leads the diamond suit first, she will have to allow you to win the ♦ K and maybe even the ♦ 10 before she can run the suit. She will have to give you the lead back and you can continue to attack the heart suit. Lead the ♥ Q.

The Opponents Have Used Stayman

Stayman is a convention that is used by the responder to an opening bid of 1NT. To use the Stayman convention, the responder must have at least 8 high-card points and four cards in one or both of the major suits. When the opponents use Stayman, you can make inferences about their hands. Any bit of information you glean from the auction is helpful when you are considering an opening lead.

Here is the auction:

WEST	NORTH	EAST	SOUTH
	Pass	1NT	Pass
2 ♣	Pass	2 ♠	Pass
3NT	Pass	Pass	Pass

Consider your options. East has 15–17 high-card points. When West bid 2 ♣, he was asking his partner to bid a major suit if he had one. The 2 ♣ bid is totally artificial when they are playing Stayman.

> When the opponents use a convention—in this case, Stayman—you overhear their auction. Since they are using the 2 ♣ bid as an artificial bid that says nothing about the club suit, you or your partner can use the double bid to show a natural club suit for your side. When your partner doubles an artificial 2 ♣ bid, then you should lead clubs.

Why is West using Stayman? Because West has at least one major suit with four cards and at least 8 HCP (high-card points). Their goal is to find a fit in one of the major suits. West is asking the question, "Do you have a four-card major?"

When East bid 2 ♠, he was saying, "I have four cards in the spades suit, and 15–17 high-card points." West concludes the bidding for the opponents with a 3NT bid.

If West also had four cards in the spade suit, he would have been interested in playing in a final spade contract. What do you know? West has four cards in the heart suit and enough high-card points to play in game opposite the 1NT opening bid.

With that information, consider your opening lead with each of the following hands.

♠ K872
♥ Q76
♦ A10
♣ J1074

The declarer has four cards in the spade suit, and the responder (the dummy) will have four cards in the heart suit. That information eliminates either of those suits from being led. The doubleton in diamonds makes that a bad lead against no-trump, so your best choice is a club. The fourth-best card in the club suit is the ♣ 4. By the process of elimination, you have found the best lead from your perspective.

♠ KQ109
♥ K974
♦ 1097
♣ Q5

There is no sure-fire lead on this hand. Your spades are good enough to lead in spite of the auction. If you choose a spade, lead the ♠ K. Some players might lead the fourth-best heart, thereby forcing a high card to be played from dummy. A club would be a terrible lead, and the diamond might find your partner with an honor or two. Nothing is clear-cut on this hand; sometimes you have to make a guess.

♠ KQJ93
♥ A5
♦ 942
♣ 942

Lead the ♠ K. Sometimes your suit is good enough to lead even though you know the declarer has four of them. The declarer probably has the ♠ A. If he doesn't have the 10 to go with it, you will take four tricks in the suit with ease.

Leads Against Competitive No-Trump Contracts

In a competitive auction when your partner has bid, there are rules you should consider. You have options and you are reviewing them in light of the information from the auction. Your first option is to lead your partner's suit. This is often a very productive lead. Your partner has bid the suit for a reason, and you must oblige and lead the suit.

Productive Leads

Productive leads in your partner's suit against no-trump contracts are the following:

- When holding two cards in partner's suit, lead the higher of the two.
- When holding three low cards, lead low unless you have raised partner's suit during the auction. If you raised, lead the middle card or a high card. If you haven't raised, leading a high card might cause partner to play you for a doubleton.
- When holding touching honors, lead the higher of the honor cards.
- When holding four cards with an honor card, lead the fourth best.
- With two touching honors in a three-card holding, lead the higher of the honors.

The only reason you won't lead your partner's suit is when you have a significant suit of your own. Your suit should be five cards long and headed by a at least three honors, perhaps KQ J. Only then will you lead your suit in preference to your partner's suit.

But you won't lead your suit if the opponents have bid that suit. Your suit must be solid, very solid, if you intend to lead your suit when the opponents have bid that suit.

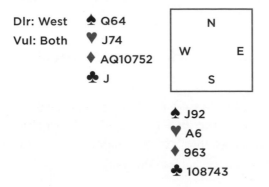

Dlr: West
Vul: Both

♠ Q64
♥ J74
♦ AQ10752
♣ J

♠ J92
♥ A6
♦ 963
♣ 108743

East is the declarer. In this auction your partner has bid hearts. The West hand is the dummy. The opponents bought the contract for 3NT (you will see that 3NT is not a good contract, but that's not the point). Lead the ♥ A, win the trick, and then lead the ♥ 6. You are leading the ♥ A so that your partner can win the next trick in hearts.

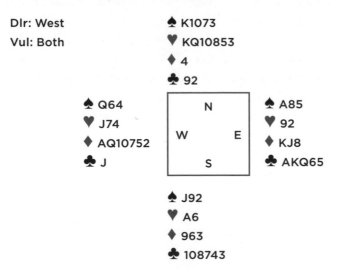

Dlr: West
Vul: Both

♠ K1073
♥ KQ10853
♦ 4
♣ 92

♠ Q64
♥ J74
♦ AQ10752
♣ J

♠ A85
♥ 92
♦ KJ8
♣ AKQ65

♠ J92
♥ A6
♦ 963
♣ 108743

Your partner is delighted to see the ♥ A. When you continue the suit, your partner will win and run six tricks. If you lead any other suit, the opponents will take the first twelve tricks. If you lead the ♥ 6, your partner will win and return a heart. You will have to win with the ♥ A, and your side will win only two tricks. What a difference a lead makes.

♠ 85
♥ AJ107
♦ K10974
♣ 73

In this case, lead your own longest suit. Your heart cards should win tricks when the opponents lead that suit, and you can continue to lead diamonds. Start out with the ♦ 7. Each and every time you get in—that is, when you win a trick—continue to lead diamonds. With any luck, your partner will have something in diamonds to help you develop tricks in the suit.

♠ QJ9
♥ J4
♦ AK642
♣ 732

Lead the ♦ A on this hand. You have touching honors and most of the points for your side. When you see the dummy after you win this trick you will have some idea of the lie of the suit. When you have touching honors, lead the higher of the honors.

♠ AQ962
♥ 764
♦ 76
♣ K64

Lead the fourth-best card from your longest suit against no-trump. In this case, you will lead the ♠ 6. If your partner has as little as the jack and two low spades, your side could win four tricks in this suit.

♠ 6532
♥ KQJ10
♦ 10853
♣ 9

Your only hope for winning tricks with this hand is to lead the top of a sequence, or touching honors. Lead the ♥ K. If your partner can win a trick she will lead back a heart, and your hand will produce three tricks for your side.

♠ KJ1093
♥ 74
♦ K83
♣ QJ10

The declarer bid spades during the auction. Do not lead that suit. Instead, lead the ♣ Q. Your intent is to play a waiting game and let the declarer lead the spades later and get the bad news. You have the benefit of attacking the club suit and waiting to spring the trap on the hapless declarer.

What Not to Lead Against No-Trump

There are leads you should never make against a no-trump contract. Do not lead a suit that was bid by either of the opponents. You are literally playing into their hand if you do. (Bridge is the origin of that little cliché.) You will be giving tricks away. Leave that suit for the declarer to lead during the play. Let the declarer find out that you have honor cards in her suit.

In general, it is not a good idea to lead a singleton against a no-trump contract. All you are doing is helping the declarer set up a long suit. With no better choice, it is okay to lead the singleton if your partner has bid the suit strongly. Your order of preference for leading against a no-trump contract in a competitive auction is to lead your partner's suit, or lead a suit of your own. If you were in the auction, and you bid a suit and your partner raised the suit, then, by all means, lead that suit.

Defeating no-trump contracts takes partnership cooperation. If you lead from your longest suit and your partner wins a trick later in the play, you should expect your partner to return your suit if she can. You must do the same. If your partner leads a suit, you should look to return it later in the play. Never lead an honor card unless it is part of a sequence (KQ , Q J, J10, etc.). Even if your partner bid the suit, do not lead an honor unless it is from a doubleton holding. With three or four to an honor in your partner's suit, lead low.

When the opponent has bid your suit, and your partner has not bid, then lead from a worthless three-card holding. In this case lead the top of nothing.

If you have a four-card suit with broken sequences, such as KJ108, lead the jack. The jack has a better chance of forcing out an ace than does the 8. If you have a broken sequence with the two cards higher than the 9 or 10, then lead the 9 or 10.

If you remember nothing more than the three most important options against a no-trump contract, then you will do just fine:

1. First, lead your partner's suit.
2. Second, lead the fourth-best from your longest suit.
3. Third, lead the unbid suit. In such a case, the opponents have gotten to 3NT and have not bid hearts, and you have four of them. Lead a heart.

When looking at a hand and deciding what to lead, it is often good to consider what not to lead. By eliminating the worst leads immediately, the right lead will be easier to find.

PART 4

DUPLICATE BRIDGE AND RESOURCES FOR FURTHER STUDY

CHAPTER 9

WHY DUPLICATE?

You know that in your next social game you'll have a partner and two opponents, that you'll deal out the cards, conduct an auction, fight it out with the opponents for your tricks, then toss the cards in a pile to be shuffled so you can start the next deal. However, there is a completely different way of playing bridge—a style that many players find infinitely more satisfying. Welcome to the world of duplicate.

Duplicate Basics

In the twenty-first century, everyone plays contract bridge. You may play bridge for money, known as "rubber bridge." You may prefer to play only at home with the neighbors. This is usually called "party bridge." If you discover duplicate at a club or a tournament, that may be your preference. No matter which way of playing bridge you favor, however, each is a form of contract bridge. Many people who are unfamiliar with duplicate bridge believe it is different from contract bridge. The method of scoring and the strategies are different, but it's still contract bridge.

Who Plays Duplicate?

Anyone with a bit of a competitive streak is a natural for duplicate. The mechanics of duplicate will be explained later in this chapter. For now, it's important to know that duplicate is a more competitive game than party bridge, but don't make the mistake of assuming there is no social element to duplicate.

On the contrary, bridge clubs are typically the most social of gathering places, and many people enter the duplicate arena with a desire to make new friends and find new partners as much as they do for the thrill of competition.

Duplicate bridge is so called because the deals are played over and over. Hands are not thrown in and shuffled each time they are bid and played. The deals are preserved in special trays and moved from table to table to be played up to thirteen times in one session.

The 170,000 members of the American Contract Bridge League, which is the sanctioning body for tournaments in North America, run the gamut of occupations and experience levels. The ACBL conducts three major tournaments each year—in the spring, summer, and fall— and you can find players who are just starting out playing at the same tournament as world champions. They don't play against one another, of course, because there are games for all levels of players.

The three big tournaments last eleven days and attract top experts from around the world. The ACBL also sanctions more than a thousand tournaments of various levels and sizes. Just about anywhere you live, there will be several tournaments a year within easy driving distance of your home. If you live in a large metropolitan area, there may be several tournaments a year right where you live.

How It Works

As noted before, in other forms of bridge, when you finish play, the cards are thrown back in a pile and someone picks them up to shuffle so that the game can continue. The deal that was just played is gone forever. In duplicate, it doesn't happen that way. A duplicate game starts with two or three trays on the table, each of them numbered. In each tray—more commonly known as a "board"—there are four slots, one each for North,

South, East, and West. In each slot, or pocket, there are thirteen cards. To get the game going, the cards are removed from the slots, shuffled together, and dealt, but the cards are not thrown to each person at the table as you would do if you were playing at home. Instead, you deal out the cards in four piles right in front of you. When you are finished, you take the piles, each with thirteen cards, and slip them into the slots in the board. When all the dealing is done, you are ready to play.

Nowadays, many ACBL-affiliated clubs prepare the deals ahead of time using a computer for randomly dealing the cards. This allows for the production of hand records—all the deals you played in the session, with accompanying information about makeable contracts.

> When you play duplicate, your true opponents are not the players you are sitting with at the table. Your true opponents are the pairs who are playing the same direction you are. If you are East–West, your scores will be compared to the other East-West pairs, even though you are playing against North-South players during the session. It is the East-West pairs whose scores you want to beat.

You noticed when you started out that you were sitting in one of the compass directions. You will keep that seat throughout the session. If you are playing East–West with your partner, you will be moving from table to table throughout the session. If you are North–South, you get to stay at the table where you started.

Each table in a duplicate game has a place card on it with a number. With a ten-table game, the tables would be numbered one through ten. The number of the table you start at is your number for the entire session. If you are playing East–West and start out at table one, you are pair number one. You will see why this is important as the game of duplicate is explained further.

Don't Mix 'Em

In duplicate, the cards are not mixed together the way you learned to do it for social or rubber bridge. When you play a card in duplicate, you place it on the table in front of you, and it stays there. When the next player sees that you have played, she places the card she wishes to play on the table in front of her. As the declarer, you would call a card for the dummy to play, and your partner would pick that card up and place it in front of her. Finally, the last person to play would place a card on the table, completing the trick.

You and the opponents continue this way until all thirteen tricks have been played. The cards are never mixed together.

So how do you keep track of which tricks you won and which tricks you lost?

It's easy: if you win the trick, you place it down on the table in a vertical position—that is, straight up. If you lose the trick, you place the card horizontally. Each player does this throughout the deal.

When the deal is complete, you determine how many tricks you took and make sure everyone is in agreement on that issue, then each player picks up the thirteen cards in front of him or her and replaces the cards in the correct slot in the board. (If for example you are East, you return your cards to the East slot.) Each board, besides having a number, also has the compass directions on the top of the tray to assist players.

All this may sound complicated and difficult, but in no time at all you will find that it is second nature. You won't even have to think about what you're doing after only two or three deals.

The Lure of Masterpoints

A common question asked by non-bridge players of those who play at duplicate clubs or at tournaments is: what do you get if you win?

The answer is usually mystifying: masterpoints. What are they? Can you spend them at the supermarket or turn them in for valuable prizes?

No, but tens of thousands of people lust after them just the same. In fact, the masterpoint is the stock in trade of the American Contract Bridge League, the world's largest bridge organization, and its cousin, the American Bridge Association. Most bridge organizations in foreign countries reward their members' bridge achievements with masterpoints.

A masterpoint is a measure of achievement in bridge competition. Bridge clubs might have a jackpot of a few dollars, but there are no cash prizes for winning, nor are there at tournaments, even at large ones. The currency is masterpoints.

One of the ACBL's principal duties is to award and keep track of the masterpoints awarded to each and every member. This is done by player numbers. Whenever you play at a bridge club or enter a tournament, your player number—unique to you—is entered so that if you do well, you will receive proper credit.

Scoring Differences

It is vital that you keep your cards from getting mixed up with other players' cards because of the way the scoring is done in duplicate.

Take that same 4 ♥ contract. If you bid and make it, you get your 120 as in regular bridge, but you also get a bonus tacked on right away: 300 if you are not vulnerable, 500 if you are. So your score for that one deal would be 420. If you happened to make an overtrick you would get the 150 plus your bonus, 450 or 650 depending on your vulnerability.

With part scores, it's a different matter. Say you bid 2 ♠ and make it on the nose. You would get your 60—two times 30 for two tricks over the basic six—but you would also get a bonus of 50 points for making your contract. Your total would be 110.

Say you had a bidding mishap and stopped in 2 ♠ when you should have been in 4. You must bid your game to get credit for it, but you do get plus 120 for the tricks and the bonus of 50 for making your contract. That's plus 170.

If you bid to game, you get the game bonus but not the 50-point bonus for making your contract.

There are slam bonuses as well (higher if you are vulnerable) and a special bonus of 50 points if you make a doubled contract. The various scores are usually on the back of that table card mentioned earlier—the one with the number on it and the compass directions.

Pairing Up

Most of the duplicate games you will find at clubs, and the majority of the games you will experience at tournaments, are pairs games. That is, the contestants are all divided up into partnerships or pairs. It's you and your partner against everyone else.

In a regular bridge game, scoring is on "total points." In duplicate, all the pairs are competing for matchpoints. From start to finish in a duplicate game, the North player fills out score tickets that reflect what happened on that particular round. Most duplicate games are played with two or three deals per round.

Many clubs today use electronic scoring through a device that sits on the table. When the auction is completed, the North player enters the contract and the compass position of the declarer. When play is finished on that deal, North enters the result in the device. The information is sent electronically to a computer that produces the scores for each deal and the scores for each pair.

The highest plus score available in duplicate bridge is for the contract of 1NT redoubled, scoring all thirteen tricks—3,160. The highest minus score also involves the taking of all thirteen tricks by the defense in a redoubled contract—7,600.

When the auction is completed, the North player writes down the contract and who is playing it, such as 3NT by West. When the play on that deal is completed, North will record the result. If 3NT is successful, East–West will get a plus score. If 3NT fails, North–South will get the plus.

After each round is completed, the director picks up the score slips and punches the information into a computer equipped with software especially designed for bridge games.

When all play is completed and all the scores from all the tables have been entered into the computer, the director pushes the button to score it all and the software spits out the final product: all the scores of all the pairs in the game. The East–West pairs are ranked together, as are the North–South pairs.

Comparisons

You might think all these scores you've been getting have been piling up in the computer and are ready to come tumbling out, with your minus scores subtracted, of course. But, it doesn't work that way.

Your score will be based on comparisons: how you and your partner did on each deal compared to the results achieved by all the other pairs who played the same deals. Let's look at a typical deal from a typical game.

Suppose there were ten tables in play. In most ten-table games, there would be three boards per round and a total of nine rounds. What follows is the story of Board 1.

Here's how matchpoints work. If you and your partner are playing North–South, you will get your score by comparing how you did on each of the deals to the score achieved by each of the other North–South pairs. For each pair you beat, you received 1 matchpoint. You received ½ matchpoint for all pairs you tie.

DUPLICATE GAME			
CONTRACT	PAIR	SCORE	MATCHPOINTS
4 ♠	1N–S	+420	3
4 ♠	10N–S	+420	3
4 ♠	9N–S	+450	6.5
3NT	8N–S	+430	5
3 ♠	7N–S	+170	1
4 ♠ X	6N–S	+590	8
5 ♠	5N–S	–50	0
4 ♠	4N–S	+420	3
4 ♠	3N–S	+450	6.5

Looking at the chart more closely, here's what happened. Starting with the top score of plus 590, North–South Pair 6 got to the game, and for some reason one of the players of the East–West pair thought it was a poor contract, thus the double (as noted by X). In duplicate, when you play a doubled contract, you get double your regular score plus 50 for making a doubled contract, plus the game bonus.

So on that score, it would be 240 (double the usual 120), plus 50 for making a doubled contract, plus the non-vulnerable game bonus of plus 300. Add them up and you have plus 590.

Going back to the chart explaining Board 1, North–South Pair 6 scored plus 590. That was better than eight other scores on that board, so their matchpoint score was 8.

Looking further, we see that Pair 3 and 9 managed to take eleven tricks in 4 ♠ and thus recorded plus 450: five tricks over the basic six at 30 points per trick, plus the 300-point bonus for bidding game. Plus 450 was better than six other scores, but two pairs achieved the score, so they received an additional ½ matchpoint for the tie. Thus their scores were 6.5.

North–South Pair 8 arrived at the unusual contract of 3NT and they took the same ten tricks as most of the other pairs in spade contracts, but the extra ten points for the first trick in no-trump gave them an edge. At plus 430, they score better than five other pairs, so their matchpoint score is a 5.

> When you make a doubled contract, you received a bonus of 50 points to go with the other scores. In bridge parlance, the 50-point bonus is often articulated this way after the other scores have been noted: "...and 50 for the insult."

You can see that three pairs played in 4 ♠ and made it on the nose for plus 420. They were better than the plus 170 and the minus 50, and they each received an extra point for tying two other pairs, so their score was 3.

Now we come to the pair who had a bidding misunderstanding and stopped short of game at 3 ♠. They made ten tricks, but since they didn't bid the game, they don't get the game bonus. Their score of plus 170 was better than only one other pair—the minus 50—so they receive only 1 matchpoint.

Pity North–South Pair 5. They got too high, bidding up to 5 ♠, and the opponents took three tricks. For minus 50, they got no matchpoints because their score was not higher than any other pair's. They received what is known in the duplicate world as a "zero," or a "goose egg." Conversely, the pair who were doubled in 4 ♠, and made it, got what is known as a "top"—the top score available.

Minus Can Be Good
You will note that you don't have to have a plus score in duplicate to score a lot of matchpoints. Suppose, for example, that you open 1NT, everyone passes, and after the opening lead the dummy comes down with almost nothing. You know you have no chance to make your contract, but

if you can hold the minus score to a smaller number than the other pairs playing the same hand you are holding now, you can get a good score.

Say in this 1NT contract you are really clever and manage to go down only two tricks for minus 100, while at every other table the declarers went down at least three, sometimes more. In that event, with the lowest minus score, you would receive the same top as if you had actually made your contract.

In duplicate, the margin of the excess is not important. What is important is to have the highest plus score or the lowest minus score. In other words, if you are playing North–South and make plus 110 for bidding and making 2 ♠ while every other North–South pair gets plus 100 for beating their opponents in some contract, you will score the same top as if you egged your opponents into bidding to some high contract and then doubled them and collected plus 1400.

How much you beat the other scores by is not important. It's important only that you beat them or have a lower minus.

In each duplicate game, the top matchpoint score will be one less than the number of times the deal is played. In the ten-table game there would be nine rounds, so each board was played nine times. That means the best score available was eight. Each pair has eight comparisons to make. An average score is half of the maximum—in this case 4.

Why Duplicate?

When you play rubber or party bridge, you are at the mercy of the cards. If you are dealt good cards, you are a favorite to win. If you are dealt poor cards, your chances of coming out ahead are slim to none.

In duplicate, you don't need good cards to win. As explained, what you need is larger plus scores or lower minus scores. You will probably never go through a game with no plus scores or no minuses, either, but in theory you could have all minuses and still win—as long as your minuses were low enough.

Duplicate is so fascinating because, from the very beginning, you have a basis of comparison and, more important, a way to measure your progress. Say you look at the score sheet at the end of the game and note on one particular board that you got plus 110 for bidding and making 2 ♠ on the nose. You see that it was a poor score because most of the other declarers scored plus 140 for making nine tricks in a spade contract. Perhaps you will go find the board and take out all the hands—they are still there, just as they were during the play—and look at the full deal to see how you should have played to earn that overtrick. Already, you are progressing as a player.

Get the Hand Records

At most tournaments and at many clubs, there are hand records available after each session with all of the cards from all of the deals played that session, right there waiting for you to analyze to see how you might have bid or played better.

The hand records are a great way for you and your partner to review each deal, finding weaknesses in your bidding system or in your defensive play. You might take a deal you had difficulty with and ask a more experienced player what you should have done differently or how you might have played better. Perhaps the experienced player will tell you about a new way of bidding that would solve your problem. At many duplicate tournaments, there are lectures by famous players, who usually stay and answer questions. Most professional players are approachable and more than willing to help someone who is just starting out.

Duplicate Strategies

Earlier we talked about safeguarding your contract with a strategy called the "safety play." The two hands are repeated for convenience.

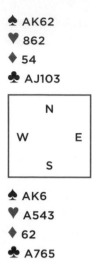

♠ AK62
♥ 862
♦ 54
♣ AJ103

♠ AK6
♥ A543
♦ 62
♣ A765

In the discussion of this contract (3NT by South), it was noted that if you play the diamonds from the top and the suit splits 4–1 instead of the expected 3–2, you will go down. You can guarantee your contract any time that diamonds split no worse than 4–1 by simply playing a low diamond from both hands on the first round of the suit. That's useful to know, but mostly irrelevant in a pairs game. There are two reasons: (1) the likelihood that the five diamonds held by the opponents will split 3–2, and (2) the importance of overtricks in a game scored by matchpoints.

When "Safe" Isn't

When you hold eight cards in a suit, the opponents hold five. The suit will split 3–2 nearly 68 percent of the time. It will split 4–1 nearly 28 percent of the time. A 5–0 split is not factored in because in this example it will mean that the contract cannot be made. If you take the safety play, you will score plus 400, which will be a great score 28 percent of the time because the other declarers will be playing diamonds from the top and going down when the suit splits 4–1. More than two-thirds of the time, however, your plus 400 will compare poorly with the other declarers because they will be scoring plus 430 with six diamond tricks, the top two spades, and the ♥ A and ♣ A. You will receive a near-bottom score for plus 400.

In Good Company

It is true that you will risk your contract by ignoring the safety play, but you must consider that the other declarers will be doing the same thing, and when the diamond suit breaks poorly they will be minus the same as you are. In fact, it's conceivable that on this deal minus 50 could be an average score. True, you will get a top on the occasions when the safety play comes in handy, but you will be close to a bottom more than twice as often.

Unlike total-points scoring, overtricks are very important in a game scored by matchpoints.

When to Play Safe

In normal contracts such as the one in the example, you should not consider safety plays. There are occasions, however, when playing safe to make your contract is the only way to go. A prime example would be when you are in a doubled contract. Let's change this example contract around a bit:

♠ AK62
♥ 862
♦ 54
♣ AJ103

```
        N
   W         E
        S
```

♠ 54
♥ A43
♦ AKQ1076
♣ 76

WEST	NORTH	EAST	SOUTH
	1 ♣	1 ♥	2 ♦
Pass	2 ♥	Dbl	2NT
Pass	3NT	Dbl	All Pass

Your partner's 2 ♥ bid was checking to see if you had a stopper in hearts. East doubled that bid to confirm with his partner that he wanted a heart lead. You showed your stopper by bidding 2NT and your partner went to game. East was not convinced that you can make nine tricks, so he doubled.

West led the ♥ 9, and East played the jack. You played low, and East continued with the ♥ K. You played low again, and West showed out. East played a third round of hearts, knocking out your only stopper in the suit. Now what? Clearly, you can make ten tricks if the diamond suit splits normally, but what if East has four to the jack? If you play the suit from the top, on the fourth round East will get in and cash a bunch of hearts to defeat you in a doubled contract.

It isn't any better if West has four diamonds to the jack. Say you play the suit from the top and give a diamond to West. She won't have any more hearts to play to East, but you won't have any way to your hand to enjoy those now-good diamonds. Your ♥ A is gone, remember.

The solution? Go to the dummy with a spade and play a diamond to your 10. Assuming East follows, West can win the jack if she has it, but she has no heart to play to her partner. You can win the return and play that low diamond in dummy to your hand, racking up your nine tricks and a doubled contract. For the record, making 3NT doubled is 550—750 if you are vulnerable.

Either score will be a clear top. If you made the overtrick, you would have scored plus 650 or plus 950, but you don't need the overtrick in this case because of the foolish double by East.

CHAPTER 10

RESOURCES TO IMPROVE YOUR GAME

This book has given you a basic education in bridge, but there's always room for more knowledge. I've spent decades playing bridge and writing about it, and I'm always aware of how much I don't know about the game. The resources listed in this chapter are a starting point for your further education in the art of bridge.

Bridge-Related Websites

American Bridge Association
http://ababridge.org

American Contract Bridge League
World's largest bridge organization. Myriad features, information, bridge news, tournament calendars, and free "Learn to Play Bridge" software. www.acbl.org

Baron Barclay Bridge Supply
World's largest bridge supply house. www.baronbarclay.com

Bridge Base Online
Free site with a wide variety of information, tutorials, and quizzes. www.bridgebase.com

Bridge Blog List
List of numerous blogs by well-known experts and aspiring players. Wide variety of topics.
www.clairebridge.com/category/blogs/

Canadian Bridge Federation
http://cbf.ca

ECatsBridge
From Great Britain, lots of information about bridge.
www.ecatsbridge.com

Great Bridge Links
Canadian site with dozens of useful links.
http://greatbridgelinks.com

Karen's Bridge Library
Comprehensive list of bridge books for advanced players.
www.kwbridge.com

World Bridge Federation
Umbrella organization for more than one hundred bridge organizations throughout the world. Puts on all world championships, promotes bridge.
www.worldbridge.org

Personal Websites

Phillip Alder
Syndicated columnist and teacher.
www.bridgeforeveryone.com

Larry Cohen
Top player and author.
www.larryco.com

Jeff Hand
National champion and teacher.
www.realbridgehands.com

Eddie Kantar
Another well-known name in bridge.
www.kantarbridge.com

Mike Lawrence
One of bridge's most popular authors.
http://michaelslawrence.com

Migry Zur Campanile
Editor of *Israeli Bridge* magazine. US national champion who now resides in America.
www.migry.com

Online Bridge Play

Bridge Base Online
By far the largest online service. Games around the clock, including dozens of ACBL masterpoint games weekly.
www.bridgebase.com

OKbridge
Also has many ACBL masterpoint games.
www.okbridge.com

Swan Games

Some ACBL masterpoint games.

www.swangames.com

Bridge Magazines

The Bridge Bulletin

Included with membership in the ACBL. Articles on improving bidding and play, tournament schedules, tournament reports, personality profiles, features on new players.

The Bridge World

Venerable publication more for experienced players and experts. Can be esoteric. Challenge the Champs (bidding contest) and Master Solvers (bidding problems) each month.

Recommended Books

American Contract Bridge League. *Laws of Duplicate Bridge*. ACBL, 2008.

Bergen, Marty. *More Points, Schmoints!* Bergen Books, 1999.

Bergen, Marty. *Points, Schmoints!* Bergen Books, 1995.

Berkowitz, David, and Brent Manley. *Precision Today*. DBM Publications, 2002.

Bird, David, and Tim Bourke. *Saints and Sinners*. Master Point Press, 2000.

Blackwood, Easley. *Card Play Fundamentals*. Devyn Press, 1986.

Grant, Audrey. *An Introduction to Bridge Bidding*. The Club Series. American Contract Bridge League, 1994.

Grant, Audrey. *Introduction to Bridge: Play of the Hand*. The Diamond Series. American Contract Bridge League, 1999.

Hamman, Bob, and Brent Manley. *At the Table: My Life and Times.* DBM Publications, 1996.

Hardy, Max. *The Problems with Major Suit Raises and How to Fix Them.* Devyn Press, 1998.

Hardy, Max. *Two over One Game Force.* Devyn Press, 2006.

Horton, Mark. *The Mammoth Book of Bridge.* Carroll & Graf, 2000.

Kantar, Edwin B. *Introduction to Declarer's Play.* Wilshire Books, 1990.

Kantar, Edwin B. *Roman Keycard Blackwood.* Robert Hale Limited, 2001.

Kantar, Edwin B. *Take Your Tricks.* Second Edition. Squeeze Books, 2008.

Kantar, Edwin B. *Test Your Bridge Play.* Wilshire Books, 1981.

Kelsey, Hugh. *Killing Defence at Bridge.* Houghton Mifflin, 1994.

Kelsey, Hugh. *Simple Squeezes.* Houghton Mifflin, 1995.

Klinger, Ron. *Playing to Win at Contract Bridge.* Orion, 1999.

Lawrence, Michael. *The Complete Book on Balancing in Contract Bridge.* Max Hardy, 1981.

Lawrence, Michael. *The Complete Book on Hand Evaluation in Contract Bridge.* Devyn Press, 1993.

Lawrence, Michael. *The Complete Guide to Passed Hand Bidding.* Second edition. Lawrence & Leong, 1993.

Lawrence, Michael. *How to Play Card Combinations.* Devyn Press, 1989.

Lawrence, Michael. *How to Read Your Opponents' Cards.* Devyn Press, 1991.

Lawrence, Michael. *Judgment at Bridge 2.* Baron Barclay Bridge, 2017.

Lawrence, Michael. *Mike Lawrence's Workbook on the Two over One System.* Baron Barclay Bridge, 2006.

Love, Clyde. *Bridge Squeezes Complete.* Dover, 1968.

Mahmood, Zia. *Bridge My Way.* Granovetter, 1992.

Manley, Brent. *The Tao of Bridge*. Adams Media, 2005.

Mollo, Victor. *I Challenge You*. Fireside, 1988.

Mollo, Victor, and Nico Gardener. *Card Play Technique*. Batsford, 1955; reissue, 2002.

Root, William. *The ABCs of Bridge*. Three Rivers Press, 1998.

Roth, Alvin. *Picture Bidding*. Granovetter, 1992.

Seagram, Barbara, and Marc Smith. *Bridge: 25 Ways to Compete in the Bidding*. Master Point Press, 2000.

Sheinwold, Alfred. *Five Weeks to Winning Bridge*. Permabooks, 1962; reissue, Pocket Books, 1996.

Simon, S. J. *Why You Lose at Bridge*. Pomona Press, 2008.

Sontag, Alan. *The Bridge Bum*. Master Point Press, 2003.

Stewart, Frank. *Better Bridge for the Advancing Player*. Prentice Hall, 1984.

Stewart, Frank. *Frank Stewart's World of Bridge*. Squeeze Books, 2008.

Stewart, Frank. *Keys to Winning Bridge*. Stewart, 2017.

Stewart, Frank. *My Bridge and Yours*. Stewart, 1992.

Wolff, Robert. *The Lone Wolff: Autobiography of a Bridge Maverick*. Master Point Press, 2008.

American Bridge Association

American Bridge Association, based in Atlanta. Membership of about five thousand.

ACBL

American Contract Bridge League, based in Horn Lake, Mississippi, near Memphis, Tennessee. World's largest bridge organization at approximately 170,000 members.

GLOSSARY

advance The first move made by the partner of a player who overcalls. The player who makes that first move is called the "advancer."

arrangement The method of separating one's cards, usually in alternating black and red suits.

artificial bid A bid that does not denote a holding designated by that bid.

asking bid A bid that requests information from the partner of the player using the bid. Examples are Stayman and Blackwood.

attack Usually associated with opening leads, an attack implies an aggressive position, which incurs some risk.

attitude On defense, one player's position regarding a play by his or her partner. This is expressed by the cards played, never by facial expression, gesture, or comment.

auction The process of deciding on the final contract via the bidding.

auction bridge The predecessor to contract bridge.

average In duplicate bridge, exactly half of the maximum score attainable.

avoidance The process of keeping a particular opponent off lead, usually to prevent a play through a particular card, such as a king.

balance Action aimed at keeping the auction from dying at a low level, usually based on the assumption that high-card points are fairly evenly divided between the two sides.

balanced hand A hand with no singleton and no more than one doubleton. There are three balanced patterns: 4-3-3-3, 4-4-3-2, or 5-3-3-2.

bid A call that offers to win a certain number of tricks in the denomination named.

bidder A player who makes a bid.

bidding space The amount of "space" in terms of bids which can no longer be made. All bids must be higher than previous bids. An opening bid at the three level uses "space" by precluding all bids at the one and two levels.

Biritch A Russian card game from which the name of the game of bridge is said to have been derived.

Blackwood A bid, usually of 4NT, requesting that the bidder's partner indicate in steps how many aces she holds in her hand.

blank Another way of denoting a void—no cards in the suit.

board In duplicate, a reference to the tray used to hold the hands. The tray moves from table to table during a game.

book The first six tricks won in the play of any contract. These tricks do not count in the score.

bottom In duplicate, the lowest possible score on a deal—a zero.

break The layout of opposing cards in a suit. Five outstanding cards rate to "break" 3–2 most of the time.

bridge whist The forerunner of auction bridge.

broken sequence A combination of at least three high cards with two of them in sequence, such as AQ J or KJ10.

buy Being successful in a competitive auction, as in, "He bought the contract for 3 ♠."

call Any bid, pass, double, or redouble. All bids are calls, but not all calls are bids.

captain In a team event, the player designated to turn in scores and to determine who plays.

captaincy A principle that states that the first player to make a limit bid cedes captaincy to her partner. Once one player has limited her hand during the auction, the other player is presumed to know how high the two hands should go. His decisions must be respected.

cash To play a winning card.

cash in To take tricks by playing winning cards one after another, usually as a last chance. Also articulated as "cash out."

cheapest bid The bid that takes up the least amount of space from the previous bid, as 1NT after 1 ♠, or 2 ♦ after 2 ♣.

claim To shorten play, usually done by the declarer, when it is clear the defenders can take no more tricks. It is sporting to claim rather than play on when there is no point to it, but claiming can be dangerous if not accurate. Best avoided by new players.

clear a suit In no-trump play, to force out high cards held by the opponents so that the remaining cards in the suit are good.

club The lowest-ranking suit (♣). Also, a place where bridge is played.

coffeehousing To indulge in unethical actions intended to mislead the opponents, usually by mannerism.

come-on Usually a signal accomplished by a sequence of card plays that indicates a desire for a suit to be continued (see echo and high-low).

comparison The method of determining scores in duplicate bridge (see IMP and matchpoint).

compass points The positions of the four players, particularly at duplicate. East–West always play as partners, as do North–South.

contract The designation of the target number of tricks for the declaring side in a particular denomination.

convention A call or play with a particular meaning, such as Blackwood 4NT or fourth-best opening leads.

convention card In duplicate, a preprinted card that is filled out according to a partnership's agreements as to conventions, bidding system, and defensive carding.

count To keep track of high-card points and cards in the four suits.

crossruff To use trumps in each hand to ruff losing cards from the other hand.

cuebid A forcing bid that normally is not offered as a possibility for play, especially the bid of an opponent's suit. A cuebid often indicates a control, such as an ace or void, in a suit.

deal To distribute all fifty-two cards, and the entire deck once the cards have been dealt. A hand is thirteen cards; a deal is fifty-two cards.

dealer The player who distributes the cards and who is the first to call in the auction.

deception The deliberate attempt to mislead an opponent, usually by the declarer, but only by the card played, not by the manner in which it is played (as with a hesitation aimed to deceive).

declarer The player who was first to name the denomination of the final contract. The declarer controls the plays made by the dummy.

defeat To prevent the declarer from making his or her contract.

defender Either opponent when the other side has won the contract.

defense The process of attempting to prevent the declarer from winning enough tricks to make his or her contract. Defense is said to be the most difficult part of the game of bridge.

defensive bidding The actions taken by partners after the opponents have opened the bidding. Also known as "competitive bidding."

diamond The second-lowest suit in rank (♦).

director In duplicate, the person who runs the game, usually entering scores and ruling on irregularities, such as leads out of turn.

distribution How the cards are dispersed in a given suit among the four hands.

double A call that increases the scoring value of contracts that are made— or of penalties for defeated contracts.

double finesse A finesse against two honors, such as playing the 10 when leading up to the AQ10, hoping the king and jack are both on the left.

double raise Skipping a level of bidding in the process of raising, as in 1 ♣—P—3 ♣.

down Unsuccessful in an attempt at a contract, as in, "I was down two in 3 ♥."

draw trumps To play high trumps in an attempt to remove them from the opponents' hands.

drop-dead bid A bid that strongly suggests to your partner that there should be no more bidding.

duck To deliberately play a low card without attempting to win a trick, usually to maintain communication between hands or to deceive the declarer or a defender about the location of a particular card.

dummy The declarer's partner, and the cards held by the declarer's partner. The dummy is always exposed after the opening lead has been made.

dummy play Bridge parlance for the way in which the declarer manages the cards.

duplicate bridge The form of bridge in which scores are determined by comparisons after deals have been played again and again.

echo A signal accomplished by the play of a high card in a suit, followed by a low card (see high-low). This usually indicates interest in a continuation of the suit or of a doubleton.

empty A term usually indicating a lack of good spot cards to go with an honor, as in a suit such as A432 being called "ace empty fourth."

endplay The process of forcing an opponent to make a play to his disadvantage, such as leading away from a king into an AQ.

entry A means of moving from one hand to the other.

equals Cards in a sequence. For example, the jack is equal to the queen in a holding of Q J.

establish To make a suit or a card good, as in playing the queen, then the jack in a suit to make the 10 good.

ethics A philosophy that winning at bridge should be accomplished by fair play.

face card A king, queen, or jack.

falsecard The act of playing a card intended to deceive an opponent. The card itself.

final bid The last bid in an auction, followed by three consecutive passes.

finesse An attempt to win a trick with a lower-ranking card by taking advantage of the position of a higher-ranking card.

first hand The dealer.

five-card majors The bidding system that requires that an opening bid of 1 ♥ or 1 ♠ indicates at least five cards in the suit. This is the basis for the Standard American bidding system.

flat Another way of saying extremely balanced distribution of a single hand, usually 4-3-3-3.

follow suit The requirement that one must play a card of a suit led, if possible.

forcing Any action, including a pass, that requires further action by the player's partner.

four-card majors A bidding system of decreasing popularity in North America that permits opening bids of one of a major with only four cards. The British Acol system is based on four-card majors and a 1NT opening of 12–14 high-card points.

free bid A bid made when the obligation to bid with minimum values has been removed by an intervening action by an opponent.

gadget Colloquialism for a convention.

game bid A bid of 3NT, 4 ♥, 4 ♠, 5 ♣, or 5 ♦.

game force A bid indicating sufficient strength that neither partner is allowed to pass until a game contract has been reached.

garbage A poor hand or a hand with unsupported queens and jacks, which usually do not pull their full weight. To clarify, an "unsupported" card is one that has no other honor with it, as with Q65. An example of a "supported" queen would be Q J76.

Gerber Another ace-asking convention, usually 4 ♣, with responses being the same as for Blackwood (in steps). Used over no-trump openings and rebids.

good cards Cards that have been established in play and can be cashed.

grand slam A contract at the seven level, requiring that the declarer takes all thirteen tricks.

half trick The proposition that a particular holding will win a trick half the time.

hand records A complete record of the deals played in a session, almost always available at ACBL tournaments.

heart The second-highest-ranking suit and the symbol of the suit (♥).

high card Ace, king, queen, or jack. These have numeric values—4, 3, 2, and 1, respectively—to enable players to evaluate their hands for opening and responding purposes.

high-low A method of playing one's cards to indicate distribution and/or "attitude" about a particular suit. If you play the 9 followed by the 3 under your partner's king and ace, you are indicating you want that suit continued.

hold up To delay taking a high card, usually to disrupt communication between opposing hands or to maintain control of an opponent's suit.

holding The cards dealt in a particular suit or hand, as in, "What was your heart holding?"

honor Ace, king, queen, jack, or 10.

hook Bridge lingo for a finesse: "I made the slam by taking the heart hook."

huddle A noticeable pause in the bidding or play. To be avoided if possible because of information that can be conveyed by the break in tempo.

illegal call A call—bid, pass, double, redouble—out of rotation or of insufficient level, as 2 ♣ over 2 ♦.

IMP International matchpoint, a method of scoring team events.

impropriety An action that violates the standards of ethical conduct, such as a grimace or gesture that indicates to the player's partner unhappiness with a bid or play.

inference What is learned about your partner's hand or the opponents' hands during the bidding and play.

insufficient bid A bid that is not higher than the previous bid.

insult The penalty paid when an opponent makes a doubled contract (50 points). If the successful contract is redoubled, the penalty is 100 points.

interior sequence Cards in a sequence such as AJ109 or Q1098. The J109 and 1098 by themselves are not considered interior sequences.

invitation A bid that invites game or slam but does not commit the partnership to either.

jack The fourth-ranking card in a suit.

jump bid A bid that raises the suit at least one level higher than a simple raise: 1 ♠—P—3 ♠.

jump overcall A bid after an opponent has opened that is at least one level higher than necessary. This is usually a weak bid.

jump shift A response that jumps the bidding into a new suit: 1 ♦—P—2 ♥.

kibitz The act of watching play. A spectator is known as a kibitzer.

king The second-highest-ranking card in a suit.

knockout teams A team event, usually played with extended matches, in which the losers are eliminated.

Laws of Contract Bridge The set of rules by which the game of bridge is played. A slightly different set of rules are used for duplicate play.

lay down To put the dummy down.

laydown Descriptive term for a contract that appears to be so ironclad that the declarer can claim almost as soon as the opening lead is made.

lead The first card played after the auction is completed. The player to the left of the declarer makes the opening lead.

lead direction A call, usually a double, to indicate a strong holding in a suit and the desire for one's partner to lead that suit if the opponents win the auction.

lead up to To play a card toward a stronger holding, as from the declarer's hand to the dummy.

Life Master The rank to which most members of the American Contract Bridge League aspire.

limit bid A bid that is narrowly defined in terms of high-card points.

loser A card that cannot win a trick.

major Either of the major suits: hearts or spades.

make The action of dealing the cards, as in "make the boards," or to be successful in one's contracts, as in "She made 4 ♥."

master card The highest unplayed card of a suit.

masterpoint A measure of achievement in competition. Awarded to bridge competitors by most bridge organizations, including the ABA and ACBL.

matchpoint The means of scoring duplicate bridge pairs contests. Players earn matchpoints on every deal by comparing their scores on those deals to the scores achieved by other pairs playing the same deals.

mirror distribution A condition that exists when both partners have the same number of cards in each of the four suits.

misfit A hand in which partners have mismatched long suits and both are short in the other's long suit.

mixed pairs A duplicate contest in which all partnerships must consist of one man and one woman.

negative double A double in competition (after an overcall) that is for takeout rather than for penalty.

North The player who sits opposite South.

North American Bridge Championships One of three major tournaments put on by the American Contract Bridge League in the spring, summer, and fall. The NABC lasts for eleven days and includes contests for every level, from beginners to world champions.

no-trump A denomination in the bidding with no trump suit.

not vulnerable A condition that exposes a partnership to lower risk, but also to lower rewards, for game and slam contracts.

odds Mathematical probabilities, usually regarding suit distribution.

offside A term indicating a card is not finesseable, as with the king "behind" the AQ and therefore offside.

one no-trump A opening bid usually indicating 15 to 17 high-card points. As a response to an opening bid, 1NT usually shows a lack of trump support and a limited range of high-card points (typically 6–9).

opponent A member of the opposing side.

over One's position at the table with respect to one's right-hand opponent.

overbid To bid too much.

overcall To enter the auction with a bid after an opponent has opened the bidding.

overruff To make a trump trick by ruffing with a higher card than an opponent has used to ruff.

overtrick A trick in excess of that needed to make one's contract.

pair Two players in partnership.

pairs game A game scored by matchpoints.

par The condition that exists when both sides have done as well as possible on a particular deal.

partial Colloquial for part score.

partner The person on the other side of the table from you.

pass A call that names no denomination and indicates no desire to double or redouble at that turn.

pass out Four consecutive passes in an auction.

passout seat The position of the player whose pass will end the auction.

passive Usually applied to defensive action, a nonaggressive, safe action.

penalty The score awarded to defenders when a doubled or redoubled contract has been defeated. Also, the action taken by a director when a player has committed an irregularity, such as revoking.

penalty card A card played in error and prematurely exposed. It usually stays face up on the table.

penalty double A call aimed at increasing the penalty for an unsuccessful contract.

penalty pass A call that converts a takeout double into a penalty double, as with 1 ♥—Dbl—All Pass. The double of 1 ♥ was for takeout. Fourth hand's pass makes it a penalty double.

pianola A contract so ironclad that it is said to "play itself."

pickup slip The score slips used in duplicate pairs games.

pip The symbol indicating a suit: ♠, ♥, ♦, or ♣.

pitch Another way of saying "discard."

plain suit In a trump contract, any suit that is not trump.

pointed suit A spade or diamond.

powerhouse A very strong hand in terms of high-card points or a long, strong suit.

preemptive bid A bid that consumes a large amount of bidding space, usually with a long suit but not much high-card strength, particularly outside the long suit.

primary honors Aces and kings.

private scorecard The preprinted convention card provided at ACBL games. The card includes space for scores on the other side.

psychic bid A call, almost always a bid, that significantly misstates the high-card strength or the suit length held. Not recommended.

push In a team game, a score comparison with no difference or a difference of only 10 points. A tie.

quack The queen and jack together, usually in a useless holding.

queen The third-ranking card in a suit.

quick trick A holding that will win a trick without the need for establishment. AK together are considered two quick tricks, AQ one and a half, A or KQ together one.

raise A bid that indicates support for your partner's suit.

rebid Opener's second bid.

redouble A call following a double that further increases the penalty for an unsuccessful contract, or the reward for making it.

renege To fail to follow suit when it is possible to do so. More properly known as "revoke."

reopen Another term for "balancing."

respond To make a bid after your partner has bid or made a takeout double.

responder The partner of a player who has made a bid or takeout double.

reverse A rebid by the opener showing extra strength because the responder, in order to go back to the opener's first suit, must do so at the three level. Example: 1 ♦—P—1 ♠—P; 2 ♥.

review A summary of the bidding, starting with the opener.

rock A very strong hand; short for "rock crusher."

rotation The clockwise order in which calls and plays occur.

rounded suit A heart or club.

rubber bridge As opposed to duplicate, rubber bridge does not preserve cards for play at other tables. A rubber of bridge is complete when one side wins two games.

ruff To win a trick with a trump by using it against a plain suit.

ruff and discard Also known as ruff and sluff, it occurs when a plain suit is led and both opposing hands are void in that suit, affording the declarer the opportunity to ruff in one hand and discard from another plain suit in the other hand.

Rule of Eleven The mathematical rule applied to fourth-best opening leads, allowing the declarer and the partner of the opening leader to determine how many cards higher than the card led are held in the other hands based on the number of the card led.

Rule of Twenty A general guideline for opening bids, stating that if the high-card points and length of the two longest suits equal 20, an otherwise subminimum hand may be opened.

sacrifice To deliberately overbid, expecting to be doubled, in hopes that the penalty suffered will be less than the value of the opponent's contract.

scoring table List of the various scores for contracts, undoubled, doubled and redoubled, vulnerable and not vulnerable, all the way from 1 ♣ through 7NT.

seat A player's position at the table: North, South, East, or West.

section In a duplicate game, a group of tables designated by a letter, such as "Section A."

sequence Two or more cards in order: KQ , J10, 987, etc.

short hand Usually indicating a hand with fewer trumps than your partner's hand.

shuffle To mix up the cards preparatory to dealing.

side suit A secondary suit in one's hand.

simple finesse A play designed to surround a single card in an opponent's hand.

single raise A raise of a suit to a minimum level, as 1 ♣—P—2 ♣.

singleton One card in a suit.

slam A contract requiring the declarer to take twelve tricks (small slam) or thirteen tricks (grand slam).

spade The highest-ranking suit (♠).

spot card Any non-face card: 10 through 2.

squeeze A play that produces an extra trick by forcing an opponent to choose from among discards, all of which are bad for the defense.

Standard American A bidding system based on five-card major openings.

Stayman A convention used after a 1NT or 2NT opening to determine whether the opener has a four-card major.

stiff Colloquial term for a singleton.

stopper Cards in a suit sufficient to keep the opponents from taking all the tricks in that suit.

Swiss teams A form of duplicate in which teams of four compete in head-to-head matches, with comparisons converted to IMP for ranking purposes.

tenace Two cards not in sequence, such as AQ or KJ.

third hand The third player to bid in the auction or to make a play.

threat card Required for the successful operation of a squeeze.

throw-in play An endplay in which an opponent is put into the lead to his disadvantage.

top In duplicate, the highest score to be achieved on a deal.

trick Four cards played in rotation.

trump The suit designated by the auction.

trump support Three or more cards when the opening bid has been in a major, or if any suit has been overcalled. For minor-suit openings, trump support is usually at least four cards.

two-bid Any opening bid at the two level.

two over one response A response to an opening bid at the two level, such as 1 ♠—P—2 ♣.

two-suiter Usually a hand with two suits of at least five cards. Also sometimes applied to hands with 5–4 in two suits.

unbid suit Any suit not mentioned in the auction.

underlead To lead away from, as to lead the 2 from K542.

unfavorable vulnerability A condition existing when one side is vulnerable and the other is not. The vulnerable side is said to be at "unfavorable."

up the line Bidding at the cheapest level possible.

void No cards in a suit.

vulnerable A condition in bridge with greater rewards for game and slam bidding, and greater penalties for unsuccessful contracts.

whist A predecessor to bridge, played primarily in England.

winner A card that usually will win a trick.

working card A card is said to be working when it faces other high cards in the same suit.

yarborough A hand with no card higher than a 9.

zero In duplicate, the lowest score on a deal.

INDEX

QUICK BIDDING REFERENCE

Combined partnership HCP requirements for game and above:

- 3NT, major-suit game: 25
- Minor-suit game: 29

- Small slam in a suit: 31; in NT, 33
- Grand slam in a suit: 35; in NT, 37

▶ OPENING BIDS

Open most 12-point hands with 2 quick tricks (ace or KQ). Open all hands with 13 + 1 ♣ or 1 ♦ = 3 or more in the suit, 12–21 HCP.

With 4 in each suit, open 1 ♦; with 3 in each suit, open 1 ♣.

RESPONSES TO 1 ♣ AND 1 ♦ BY HCP

- 0–5: Pass
- 6+: Bid a 4-card major (hearts first with 4 in both)
- 6–9: Raise opener's suit to 2 (requires 4 trumps) or bid 1NT (denies 4-card major)
- 10–12: Raise opener's suit to 3 (4 trumps) or bid 2NT (denies 4-card major)

1 ♥, 1 ♠ = 12–21 HCP, 5+ in the suit.

With 5 in both, open 1 ♠ regardless of suit quality. With 16+ HCP, 5 ♥ and 4 ♣, open 1 ♥.

RESPONSES

- 0–5 HCP: Pass
- 6–9 without 3-card support: Bid 1NT (opener can pass)
- 6–9 and 3-card support: Raise to 2
- 10–12 and 4-card support: Raise to 3; with 3-card support, bid a new suit at the 2 level then show support, including a jump to game if warranted (responder has opening hand)
- 10–13 with good suit of 5+ cards, bid at 2 level

1NT = 15–17, balanced hand (no singleton or void).

RESPONSES

- 0–7 HCP with no long suit: Pass
- 0–7 with 5 or more in a major: Bid the major at the 2 level (to play); with transfers (2 ♦ = hearts; 2 ♥ = spades), transfer and pass; without transfers, 2 ♦ is to play
- 8–9 balanced: Bid 2NT (invites 3NT); with 5-card major, transfer and bid 2NT
- 8–9 with a 4-card major: Bid 2 ♣ (Stayman) to ask about 4-card majors; after opener bids a major (hearts first if holding both majors), raise to invite in the suit; 2NT invites 3NT if opener bids 2 ♦ (no 4-card major)
- 10+: Bid 3NT with no major or transfer and bid 3NT (partner corrects to the major with 3 in the suit); with 6+ in major, transfer and bid game in major
- 16–17: Bid 4NT (invites opener to bid 6NT)
- 18: Bid 6NT

Opening bids at the 2 level and higher:

2 ♣ = very strong balanced hand (22+) or a long, strong suit.

RESPONSES

- 2 ♥, 2 ♠, 3 ♣, 3 ♦ = 5+ in the suit with 2 of the top-3 honors
- 2 ♦ = "waiting" bid: Missing the honors to make an immediate positive response, but a good hand is possible
- Responder indicates a bad hand by bidding the cheaper minor after opener's rebid, e.g., 2 ♣—P—2 ♦—Pass; 2 ♠—P—3 ♣ (poor hand)

2NT = balanced hand with 20–21 HCP.

QUICK BIDDING REFERENCE

RESPONSES

- 4–10, with 4-card major, 3 ♣ (Stayman)
- 4–10 balanced or long minor, 3NT
- 4–10, 5-card major, transfer and bid 3NT; without transfers bid 3NT
- 4–10, 6+ major, transfer and bid game; without transfers, bid game in the major
- 11–12, 4NT to invite 6NT

2 ♦, 2 ♥, 2 ♠ = 6-card suit, 5–10 HCP; 2NT response asks if opener has a "feature" (ace or king); with no feature, opener bids 3 of the suit he opened.

3 ♣, 3 ♦, 3 ♥, 3 ♠ = good 7-card suit, less than an opening hand. Meant to take up opponents' bidding space. Not a strong hand.

▶ REBIDS

After opening one of a minor and a response of one of a major.

WITH 4-CARD SUPPORT

- 12–15   Raise responder's major to the 2 level*
- 16–18   Raise responder's major to the 3 level*
- 19–21   Raise responder to game in his major*

*All three of these ranges include a calculation of "support points": 1 for a side doubleton, 3 for a side singleton, 5 for a side void.

WITHOUT 4-CARD SUPPORT

- 12–15   Bid 1 ♠ if partner's response was 1 ♥
- 12–14   Bid 1NT without 4-card support
- 12–14   Rebid 2 of the minor that was opened, showing 6+ in the suit
- 16–18   Rebid 3 of the minor, showing 6+ in the suit

- 16–17   Rebid a higher-ranking suit at the 2 level (e.g., 1 ♣—1 ♠—2 ♥)
- 18–19   Rebid 2NT (denies support for responder's major but could have other major)

RESPONSES TO 4NT BLACKWOOD

5 ♣ = 0 or 4 aces

5 ♦ = 1 ace

5 ♥ = 2 aces

5 ♠ = 3 aces

5NT by the Blackwood bidder asks about kings. Responses are the same except at the 6 level. The 5NT bid guarantees that the partnership has all the aces between the two hands.

RESPONDING TO A TAKEOUT DOUBLE

After a takeout double had been made, the "advancer" (partner of the doubler) must describe his hand accurately to get to the best contract.

Example auction: 1 ♥—Dbl—P

Non-jump response (1 ♠, 2 ♣, 2 ♦) = 0–8 points

1NT = 8–10 points with stopper in opener's suit

2 ♠ = 9–11 points, 4+ spades

3 ♣ or 3 ♦ = 9–11 points, likely 5 cards in the suit

2 ♥ = cuebid to show good hand; game is close if not solid

2NT = 11–12 points with stopper

3NT = to play

Pass = strong holding in opener's suit (e.g., QJ10987); doubler normally leads a trump